D1552440

BILL ELLIOTT

"The Peaceable Man"

by Bobby J. Copeland

Published by

Empire Publishing, Inc.
PO Box 717
Madison, NC 27025-0717

Phone: 336-427-5850 • Fax: 336-427-7372
Email: movietv@pop.vnet.net

Also by Bobby J. Copeland:
Trail Talk, published by Empire Publishing, Inc.
Five Heroes, self-published
The Bob Baker Story, self-published
The Whip Wilson Story, self-published
B-Western Boot Hill, Empire Publishing, Inc.

Empire Publishing, Inc.
PO Box 717
Madison, NC 27025-0717
phone: 336-427-5850
fax: 336-427-7372
email: movietv@pop.vnet.net

Library of Congress Catalog Number 00-103634
ISBN Number 0-944019-31-5

Published and printed in the United States of America

1 2 3 4 5 6 7 8 9 0

ACKNOWLEDGMENTS AND SELECTED BIBLIOGRAPHY

Special thanks goes to Jack Mathis for his generous contribution of photographs used in the publishing of this book; to Neil Summers, for his friendship and interest in all of our publishing interests and for his willingness to share photos from his personal collection for this book and others; to Norman Foster, for the special candid photo located on page 93; and to Peggy Stewart, for sharing a few words with us about our cowboy friend Bill Elliott.

Also, special appreciation is expressed to the following (in no particular order): Paul Dellinger, John A. Rutherford, Richard B. Smith III, Joe Copeland, Rhonda Lemons, Chuck Anderson's web site, *Western Clippings, Under Western Skies, Gun World, Horse and Rider, The Old Cowboy Picture Show Newsletter, Wrangler's Roost, William Elliott and Robert Livingston* —"*The Knights of the Range*" by Mario DeMarco, *Those Six-Gun Heroes* by Douglas E. Nye, *Saturday Afternoon At the Movies* by Alan Barbour, *Tex Ritter—America's Most Beloved Cowboy* by Bill O'Neal, *The Filming of the West* by John Tuska, *Republic Confidential —Volume 2, The Players* by Jack Mathis, *Those Great Cowboy Sidekicks* by David Rothel, *A Pictorial History of the Western Film* by Willam K. Everson, *Top 100 Cowboys of the Century* by Boyd Magers, *Wild Bill Elliott* by John Leonard, *Classic TV Westerns* by Ron Jackson, *Hollywood Corral* by Don Miller, *Shoot 'em-Ups* by Les Adams and Buck Rainey, *Classic Images* article by Mike Newton, *Classic Images* article by Don Creacy, *Peggy Stewart, Princess of the Plains* by Bob Carman and Dan Scapperotti, and *Under Western Skies* article by Jim Ryan.

FOREWORD
by Peggy Stewart

I felt honored when I was asked to write the foreword for the Bill Elliott book. For almost 30 years now, I have attended the many western movie film festivals held for the fans.It has always been a privilege for me to meet and greet the fans and reminisce about the days of the silver screen cowboys. While attending these events, the name Bill Elliott will always surface in many fans' conversations. I truly believe that if a poll were taken today, Bill would be one of the top five B-Western actors of all time in the mind of today's fans.

My friend, Robert Blake, also had a special interest in talking and remembering our friend Bill. Bobby has always made it very clear that Bill Elliott was his favorite Red Ryder to work with and often refers to him as a sweet and wonderful actor. Bobby and I, after all these years, get together socially, as he lives only a few minutes drive from my home in North Hollywood.

Bill was very special; he was one of my pets. I just adored him. There was a lot of playing going on at Republic. We all teased and played around, and had a wonderful time. Bill had this wonderful, dry sense of humor, but he couldn't laugh. He had this high-pitched little hee, hee, hee—and that meant he was hysterical. Bill was so kind and courteous to everybody on the set. One thing about him I loved—he had charisma about him. At the Christmas parties, they'd open up one of the big stages . . . you knew when Elliott came into the room. It's nothing he said or anything else . . . he was just—tall, quiet—tall in the saddle. I believe everyone who worked with Bill Elliott will tell you they enjoyed it.

Bill worked hard to become a top cowboy star. He was also very business-like, and kept his own time card. He encour-

Here I am with Wild Bill Elliott in KANSAS TERRITORY (Allied Artists, 1953).

aged me to do the same. I meant to do it, but kept putting it off. One day, I received a letter from Republic's accounting department indicating I had been overpaid, and owed them $148. I knew I surely did not owe them, and took the letter to Bill. He reminded me he had told me to keep my own time, but he used his records to show the studio owed me money. It wasn't long until I received one of those "sorry about that" letters from Republic.

Bill became a fine western star—and I believe he could ride with a glass of water on his head, and never spill a drop. So relax, get comfortable, and relive a bit of history about my friend, one of the greatest movie cowboys who ever came onto a Hollywood sound stage. Wild Bill was a good friend, and I still miss him.

TABLE OF CONTENTS

WILD BILL ELLIOTT

contributed by Paul Dellinger

He would always be known as the "peaceable man"—for that, and for the way he carried his two pistols, butts forward in their holsters. But Wild Bill Elliott could never stay peaceable, and those six-guns fired their way through B-Western movie series at Columbia, Republic, and Monogram/Allied Artists before he finally hung them up.

It was legendary gunfighter James Butler "Wild Bill" Hickok who gave Elliott his movie moniker, because Elliott played Hickok in the serial that brought him to Western stardom and in several movies after that. For a while, though, he became William Elliott when Republic moved him up from B-Westerns to its higher-budgeted films.

Elliott came by none of those names naturally. He was born Gordon Nance, on a ranch in Pattonsburg, Missouri, on October 16, 1903. Nance grew up around horses, riding his first one at age five. His father was commissioner at the Kansas City stockyards, where young Nance saw many actual cowboys riding and roping. By age 16, he won first place among those cowboys in the American Royal Horse and Livestock Show. But it was a silent movie he saw at age nine that pointed him in the direction of his career. It was a movie featuring legendary Western star William S. Hart, and inspired the young viewer to want to become a cowboy star someday. Many of his later features would use the old Hart storylines of a badman who reforms.

After attending Rockingham College, Nance enrolled in the Pasadena Community Playhouse for stage performances. A talent scout signed him for movies, but few of them came any-where near Westerns. Most were society dramas, and coin-cided with his first name change to Gordon Elliott. The newly-dubbed Elliott sported a thin mustache in this phase of his career, spanning 13 years and 90 pictures starting with an appearance in a silent film, THE PLASTIC AGE (1925) star-ring Clara Bow and Gilbert Roland (a future Cisco Kid).

Elliott did appear in a few Westerns, usually on the wrong side of the law. His first ones were silents in 1928, ARIZONA WILD-CAT with Tom Mix and VALLEY OF HUNTED MEN with Jay Wilsey, better known as Buffalo Bill, Jr. By the mid-1930s, he had more prominent roles in TRAILIN' WEST (1936) and GUNS OF THE PECOS, both starring Dick Foran; ROLL ALONG COWBOY (1937) with Smith Ballew, and BOOTS AND SADDLES, where he played a bad guy brought to justice by Gene Autry.

Meanwhile, Elliott was working in just about every kind of film there was, in titles such as THE DROP KICK, RESTLESS YOUTH, PASSION SONG, THE MIDNIGHT MYSTERY, BORN TO LOVE, PEG OF MY HEART, GOLD DIGGERS OF 1933, 20 MILLION SWEETHEARTS, HERE COMES THE NAVY, DEVIL DOGS OF THE AIR, ALIBI IKE, THE STORY OF LOUIS PASTEUR, LADY IN THE MORGUE, and many more. He was in three Perry Mason mysteries: THE CASE OF THE HOWL-ING DOG, THE CASE OF THE BLACK CAT, and THE CASE OF THE VELVET CLAWS; THE SINGING KID with Al Jolson; G-MEN with James Cagney and a future frequent cowboy side-

Bill Elliott in a rare smile for the camera.

kick, Raymond Hatton; and even TARZAN'S REVENGE with Glenn Morris as the ape man.

His defining moment came in 1938 when Columbia cast him as the lead in its 15-chapter serial, THE GREAT ADVENTURES OF WILD BILL HICKOK. That was the first time he wore the reversed brace of stag-handled guns, possibly because Gary

Cooper had done so playing Hickok two years earlier in Cecil B. DeMille's THE PLAINSMAN. In fact, Hickok's show guns were ivory-handled; he wore them stuck in a sash around his waist rather than in holsters (and supplemented them with derringers and other hidden artillery; Hickok apparently believed

Here is an early shot of Wild Bill, ready for action.

in firepower), and may have killed only four men in actual gun-fights, depending on how many of the stories about him you believe. In the serial, as marshal of Abilene, Hickok takes on a gang called the Phantom Raiders. Chief Thunder Cloud, soon to become best known as Tonto, in Republic's two Lone Ranger serials, and Roscoe Ates, future comic sidekick for PRC's singing cowboy, Eddie Dean, were in the cast along with Robert Fiske as the chief villain.

Then came the next name change, to Bill Elliott, taking advantage of that identification with Hickok. But in his first starring Western feature, IN EARLY ARIZONA (1938), Columbia cast him as a lawman named Whit Gordon, and armed him with two pearl-handled six-guns worn the regular way. The story was actually one of many versions of the Wyatt Earp saga in Tombstone, Arizona, based on still more exaggerated stories about an actual frontier lawman. Jack Ingram, usually a baddie, played the lawman whose death prompts Elliott's character to clean up Tombstone and a gang led by veteran badman Harry Woods.

Continuing with the two regularly-packed guns and riding a good-looking paint horse (Elliott would go on to raise horses, and use many of his own in his future films), Columbia starred him in FRONTIERS OF '49, LONE STAR PIONEERS and THE LAW COMES TO TEXAS in 1939, then starred him in another 15-chapter serial, OVERLAND WITH KIT CARSON, with Elliott as the famed frontiersman. The serial had a disguised villain called Pegleg (who really didn't have a pegleg but somehow made it look like he did) and a murderous black stallion called Midnight, who tramples Pegleg's enemies at his command. Carson eventually tames the killer horse, and it is Pegleg who gets trampled by him in the final chapter.

By then, the pearl handles disappeared and the Hickok guns were back. Rex Allen once commented that he had wanted to be different from all his cowboy predecessors, which was why he wore a stag-handled pistol butt forward. "And then I found out that Billy Elliott did it 20 years before," he laughed. Interestingly, neither Bill or Rex resorted to a cross-draw, but would turn their gunhands around so as to jerk their pistols from the same side they were drawing from, and then flip the pistols around to drop them back in their holsters. Those butt-forward stag-handled pistols would remain Elliott's trademark for most of his career, starting with a feature called THE TAMING OF THE WEST (1939) in which he plays a hero called Wild Bill Saunders.

Elliott repeats the Saunders role in PIONEERS OF THE FRONTIER, THE MAN FROM TUMBLEWEEDS, and THE RETURN OF WILD BILL (all 1940), all climaxing in blazing shootouts and featuring a young comic sidekick played by Dub Taylor. Cannonball Taylor would later support singing cowboy Jimmy Wakely at Monogram, and go on to become a popular character actor, and father of actor Buck Taylor.

With PRAIRIE SCHOONERS (1940), Columbia dropped the Saunders gimmick, and turned Elliott into Wild Bill Hickok again, giving him a buckskin shirt to replace the square-button decor of the Saunders outfit. The paint horse, the reversed guns, and Cannonball remained, continuing through BEYOND THE SACRAMENTO (1940), ACROSS THE SIERRAS, NORTH FROM THE LONE STAR, THE WILDCAT OF TUCSON, and HANDS ACROSS THE ROCKIES (all 1941). Some of the real-life Hickok touched lightly on two of these. In ACROSS THE SIERRAS, Hickok accidentally guns down his best friend. The real Hickok actually did shoot a fellow lawman who was running to his aid when he and a gambler named Phil Coe shot it out in Dodge City, after which Hickok's career as a lawman came to an end. NORTH FROM THE LONE STAR takes place in Deadwood, where the recently-married Hickok had gone to seek gold, but, instead, got a bullet in the back from

Sneaky Ernie Adams is about to clobber Elliot in THE MAN FROM TUMBLEWEEDS (Republic, 1943).

Jack McCall, none of which happened in the movie, of course. Two small departures were taken during this series, with Elliott playing Bill Boone in THE RETURN OF DANIEL BOONE and Dave Crockett in THE SON OF DAVY CROCKETT, but the format for both was exactly the same except for the hero's name.

Columbia tried a pairing that proved immensely popular. It teamed Elliott with singing cowboy Tex Ritter, both established Western leads by this time. Ritter had just concluded a long run of singing cowboy Westerns for producer Ed Finney, initially released through Grand National, and later, by Monogram. Eight Elliott-Ritter films were released in 1941-1942, and the usual gimmick would start them out misunderstanding one another's motives and seeming to be enemies, but always ending up fighting it out with the outlaws together in the finale.

KING OF DODGE CITY and ROARING FRONTIERS were the first two film collaborations of Elliott and Ritter, and were released in 1941. The only other change was that Frank Mitchell assumed the sidekick duties from Dub Taylor. Taylor exited the Elliott films (after KING) to become the helper to Russell Hayden, the former Hopalong Cassidy pal, who was getting his own series at Columbia. Later still at Columbia Pictures, Dub Taylor was the saddle pal to Charles Starrett.

The 1942 releases began with THE LONE STAR VIGILAN-TES, followed by BULLETS FOR BANDITS, in which Elliott shoots it out with himself, in a dual role, and then impersonates the man he killed to help Tex slug it out with the baddies. He doesn't reveal himself as Hickok until it's all over, adding his by-now traditional caveat about being a peaceable man. "Yeah," Tex drawls. "I've been noticin' that." Elliott played Hickok twice more, in THE DEVIL'S TRAIL and PRAIRIE GUNSMOKE.

Bill Elliott with Tex Ritter and Shirley Patterson in NORTH OF THE ROCKIES.

In the other two Elliott-Ritter flicks, Elliott played a Mountie in NORTH OF THE ROCKIES and Mexican legend Joaquin Murietta (the only time he added the small mustache that had marked his early roles) in VENGEANCE OF THE WEST. Columbia used Elliott one last time in a third serial, THE VALLEY OF VANISHING MEN, in which he played Wild Bill Tolliver.

For the 1943-44 season, Elliott moved to Republic which is where he made probably his best pictures, and where he would eventually be elevated to A-budget features. In his first eight films, the first appropriately titled CALLING WILD BILL ELLIOTT, Elliott played a character with his own screen name for the first time. He was teamed with George "Gabby" Hayes, probably filmdom's top comic sidekick, and leading lady Anne Jeffreys who demonstrated her versatility as a schoolmarm, Indian maiden, saloon singer, and other roles. The opening film had Wild Bill and Gabby meeting for the first time, despite Gabby's tall stories to young Buzz Henry about being an old pal of Wild Bill Elliott's. Top Republic villain Roy Barcroft has his first outing against Elliott as one of a militia headed by a self-styled territorial governor. Elliott continued with the trademark firearms and paint horse, called Sonny, and a new shirt (back to the square frontal button arrangement).

Elliott and his feisty horse, Sonny in WAGON TRACKS WEST (Republic, 1943).

The winning formula continued with THE MAN FROM THUNDER RIVER, BORDERTOWN GUN FIGHTERS, WAGON TRACKS WEST, OVERLAND MAIL ROB-

BERY, DEATH VALLEY MANHUNT, MOJAVE FIREBRAND, and HIDDEN VALLEY OUTLAWS. OVERLAND MAIL ROBBERY has an unusual gang leader, a woman played by Alice Fleming (who would later portray The Duchess, aunt to Red Ryder, when Elliott moved on to that series) with two outlaw sons, played with amusing competitiveness by Barcroft and Weldon Heyburn. But the highlight is Kirk Alyn, later famous as Columbia's Superman in two serials, as a timid Bostonian whose gunshy ways make for great comedy (Alyn once said there had been plans to spin off the character in his own Western series, but it never happened), and who is also the romantic interest for Anne Jeffreys. BORDERTOWN GUN FIGHTERS has Bill and Gabby up against a gang that includes Ian Keith, Charles King, and Barcroft, but gives him Harry Woods as a competent marshal instead of a villain for a change. HIDDEN VALLEY OUTLAWS has one of the funniest lines from a crook in a B-Western, from Kenne Duncan as one of Barcroft's outlaws about to fake the murder of an actor played by Earle Hodgins. "I never did like actors," Duncan tells one of his fellow conspirators. "My wife ran off with one. But I still don't like 'em."

Just as the Hickok association with Elliott ended after Columbia, Elliott would no longer play Wild Bill anybody after HIDDEN VALLEY OUTLAWS with one exception (although he would usually be billed in the cast listing as Wild Bill Elliott). The exception was in BELLS OF ROSARITA (1945), a Roy Rogers picture in which Republic stars Sunset Carson, Bob Livingston, Allan Lane, Don Barry, and Elliott all play themselves as actors lending their fame to Roy's efforts to save Gabby's and Dale Evans' circus. The finale has the actors all actually chasing down a gang of crooks, too. Elliott chases Barcroft, and pretends to be shot by him before jumping up and clobbering him. "I'm sorry I had to do that," Elliott tells his old nemesis. "Normally, I'm a peace-loving man." Yeah, right.

Bill Elliott, Nancy Gay, and Gabby Hayes in OVERLAND MAIL ROBBERY (Republic, 1943).

Anne Jeffreys, Elliott, and Gabby Hayes. Looks like Gabby has just complained, "Durn persnickity females!"

But Elliott's new Republic series, starting around mid-1944, was as Fred Harman's comic-strip cowboy, Red Ryder. Republic had done a popular 1940 ADVENTURES OF RED RYDER serial with Don Barry, but dropped Elliott into the role for 16 movies extending into 1946. The first two, TUCSON RAIDERS and MARSHAL OF RENO, retained Gabby's comic sidekick services; thereafter, Gabby returned to a long pairing with Roy Rogers. Bobby Blake, who grew up to become actor Robert Blake, played Little Beaver, Red's young Indian side-kick, in all 16 films and Alice Fleming, as mentioned, played Red's aunt from the comic strip. The only wardrobe change was chaps for Elliott and a shirt with arrow pockets. The twin stag-handled, butt-forward guns remained, even though Harman had drawn his character in the comics as carrying only one pistol worn in traditional fashion. And Elliott began riding a black horse, Thunder, to fit Red's comic book horse. Peggy Stewart was the leading lady in the opening film, and has spoken often of what a gentleman and businessman Elliott

was. She said he was keep-
ing track of his work long be-
fore actors did so traditionally,
and advised her to do the
same. She didn't and, when
she left Republic, the studio
claimed she owed it money
from advanced payments.
She went to Elliott for help,
and he was able to use the
records he kept for himself to
show how many scenes
Stewart had performed—and
Republic ended up having to
pay her more than what she'd
already gotten. Of course, the
scenario we'd all prefer to believe is Elliott walking into the

A publicity shot of Elliott as Red Ryder.

Bill Elliott faces the camera for a shot in his Red Ryder costume.

accountants' office and saying, "Now then, I'm usually a peaceable man, but you're taking advantage of this little lady . . . ."

The third movie in the series, THE SAN ANTONIO KID, has future Cisco Kid Duncan Renaldo in the title role as a hired gun who changes sides to wipe out a gang led by Harman's continuing villain, Ace Hanlon (played by Glenn Strange; it may be worth noting that Ace Hanlon had already been killed off once, in

CONQUEST OF CHEYENNE (Republic, 1946)

the Red Ryder serial when he was played by Noah Beery, Sr.). Linda Stirling was the new leading lady, and seemed to be alternating with Peggy Stewart in future Ryder films: CHEYENNE WILDCAT, VIGI-LANTES OF DODGE CITY, SHERIFF OF LAS VEGAS (all 1944), GREAT STAGE-COACH ROBBERY (in which the respected citizen really leading the bandits is a murderous teacher, who kills one of his pupils when he learns of his deception), LONE TEXAS RANGER, PHANTOM OF THE PLAINS, MARSHAL OF LAREDO, COLORADO PIONEERS, WAGON WHEELS WESTWARD (all 1945), CALI-FORNIA GOLD RUSH, SHERIFF OF REDWOOD VALLEY, SUN VALLEY CY-CLONE, and CONQUEST OF CHEYENNE (all 1946), all fine Western films.

Elliott demonstrates his fast back-handed draw.

In WAGON WHEELS WESTWARD, Roy Barcroft plays an outlaw leader role he repeats in a later Ryder movie, VIGI-LANTES OF BOOMTOWN when Elliott was no longer in the series, possibly the only role Barcroft played twice. SHERIFF OF REDWOOD VALLEY co-stars long-time Western leading man Bob Steele as the Reno Kid, an escaped prisoner married to Peggy Stewart and trying to clear his name, which Red helps him to do. SUN VALLEY CYCLONE, though late in the series, tells the story of how Red acquired his trusty steed, and it is Thunder who sees through the disguise of outlaw Barcroft.

At that point, Republic moved Allan Lane from his Western series over to the Red Ryder role, with Bobby Blake continu-

Elliott, Blake, and Hayes in front of a large copy of a Fred Harman Red Ryder comic book.

ing as Little Beaver. The studio had bigger plans for Elliott.

Now being billed as William instead of Wild Bill, Elliott was moved up to top Western features starting with IN OLD SACRAMENTO, with Elliott as a Black Bart-style stage robber called Spanish Jack. But his love for a good woman (Constance Moore) and his effort to save the young man she loves from outlawry dooms him, and he is shot down at the conclusion.

PLAINSMAN AND THE LADY (1946) teams Elliott with Vera Ralston, girl friend and later wife of Republic studio head Herbert Yates, in a story about the Pony Express. Andy Clyde, a sidekick to both Hopalong Cassidy and

A nice shot of Elliott on his horse, Thunder.

Whip Wilson, is prominent as is Don Barry, the screen's original Red Ryder, this time as a menacing black-clad gunman on the side of wrong. Elliott may be William now, but he's back to packing his trademark butt-forward guns that he had dropped temporarily as Spanish Jack.

The next three teamed Elliott with popular leading man John Carroll, but in different kinds of roles each time. First came WYOMING (1947), with Elliott as a big rancher threatened with the loss of grazing land to homesteaders. The movie marks the last teaming of Elliott and Gabby Hayes, with Hayes playing a rancher named Windy (the name Hayes started with in his earlier sidekick roles in the "Hopalong Cassidy" series) who, no doubt to the shock of the audience, is shot and killed by one of the outlaws near the movie's end. Carroll plays Elliott's foreman, a young man who keeps trying to keep his boss from

Elliott, Bob Steele, Peggy Stewart, and Alice "The Duchess" Fleming in a publicity still for SHERIFF OF REDWOOD VALLEY (Republic, 1944).

Bill Elliott and Constance Moore in IN OLD SACRAMENTO (Republic, 1944).

getting too far outside the law. Vera Ralston plays two roles, first as Elliott's wife, and later as his daughter who is sweet on Carroll. Interestingly, at the end of the movie, Carroll adopts his boss' butt-forward twin-gun rig, only with pearl handles. Roy Barcroft has a rare, sympathetic role as a friendly sheriff.

In THE FABULOUS TEXAN (1947), Carroll's role is almost more

prominent than Elliott's in a story of corrupt state police ruling Texas. In fighting them, Carroll becomes an outlaw himself, and sacrifices his life to save Elliott's from an ambush at the end. But in OLD LOS ANGELES (1948), Carroll becomes a truly menacing badman named Johnny Morrell, who is so bloodthirsty he ends up killing the boss of his outlaw gang. He even blasts down his own girlfriend (played by Estelita Rodriguez) before Elliott finally nails him. Catherine McLeod is the new leading lady, and Andy Devine is the sidekick.

THE GALLANT LEGION (1948) has Elliott joining the Texas Rangers headed by Jack Holt and including Andy Devine. Adrian Booth almost steals the show as a newspaperwoman who rides with the rangers to tell the real story behind them. Bruce Cabot makes a strong villain.

Elliott, Booth, Devine, and Holt are re-teamed in THE LAST BANDIT (1949), the first of two Trucolor movies in which Elliott appears. Elliott plays the straight brother of outlaw Forrest Tucker. Elliott finally turns in his two-gun rig for the duration of his time at Republic, opting from now on for a single pistol, usually worn in the regular way but sometimes butt-forward.

Next came HELLFIRE (1949), Elliott's other Trucolor Western, where he plays a gambler caught with an ace up his sleeve and is nearly shot. A lay minister takes the bullet for him, and Elliott ends up promising the dying man to see that the church for which he has been working will get built - but the minister insists that Elliott do it in biblical fashion, not by cheating at cards. The first time Elliott tries to pass the hat, a man spits in it, and is promptly pounded until he apologizes. Elliott then makes his own apology for losing his temper. "The rule book says I'm supposed to be a peaceable man," he says, using that trademark phrase for the last time. Marie Windsor has an excellent role as Doll Brown, a female outlaw seeking the brothers who attacked her and her sister and being pursued by a marshal played by Tucker. She is looking for her sister, not knowing that she is Tucker's wife. Tucker wants to eliminate Doll Brown before his wife learns that she is her sister. Elliott wants Doll to give herself up to him, so he can collect the $5,000 reward and build his church. The climax has Doll choosing the Bible over her gun as she keeps the wounded marshal alive, learning that he is her brother-in-law. She takes several bullets from outlaw Jim Davis before Elliott shows up with a doctor and guns down the entire gang. We are left unsure whether Doll Brown survives to become the wife of Elliott's character.

In THE SAVAGE HORDE (1950), Elliott plays a gunfighter called Ringo who gives up his gun when he accidentally wounds his own brother (Jim Davis), a cavalry officer charged with pursuing him. The now-pacifist Elliott rides into the middle of a range war, with Bob Steele as the head gunman of a gang headed by Grant Withers and including Roy Barcroft. Adrian Booth returns as Elliott's former love interest, who is being courted by Withers until she realizes his evil intent toward the ranchers. After a shootout with Steele's character, Elliott gives himself up to the army to face whatever charges it has against him. The last thing we see is Booth watching him ride away and, again, we don't know if he will be cleared and return to her or not. Elliott's last Republic movie is THE SHOWDOWN (1950), in which he agrees to head a cattle drive for rancher Walter Brennan and investor Marie Windsor to find which member of the crew murdered his brother. The movie is full of surprises which should not be spoiled by too many details, for those who have not seen it. It was not at all a bad picture for Elliott's Republic career to end on.

In 1951, Elliott made his last studio jump to Monogram (later Allied Artists) for his last Western series, where he played different characters each time, but was once more billed in the cast as Wild Bill Elliott (complete with a return to the familiar stag-handled butt-forward pistols). THE LONGHORN has him and Myron Healey hiring ex-cons to bring herefords to Wyoming for cross-breeding. Healey, who is Elliott's rival for Phyllis Coates, is also betraying him to rustlers led by future TV Lone Ranger John Hart. But he changes sides in time to stop a bullet. Allied Artists re-made the picture in color in 1956 as CANYON RIVER, with George Montgomery and Peter Graves in the Elliott-Healey roles.

In WACO (1952), Elliott starts as an outlaw, but reforms to become a lawman, and must fight some of his old gang to save his town. KANSAS TERRITORY (1952), which reunites Elliott with Peggy Stewart, has Elliott again seeking revenge for a brother's murder. Veteran sidekick Fuzzy Knight joins the cast. FARGO (1952) has Elliott losing still another brother to Healey, an out-and-out villain this time. Coates and Knight are back in the cast.

Elliott is a cavalry officer in THE MAVERICK (1952), Healey is his sergeant, and Coates again the leading lady. THE HOMESTEADERS (1953) has Elliott hiring ex-soldiers (much as in the ex-outlaws of THE LONGHORN) to pack dynamite to his fellow homesteaders in Oregon to clear their land. This time, his betraying partner is played by Robert Lowery, but Lowery reforms in time to avoid being killed off. REBEL CITY (1953) has Elliott seeking revenge for his father's murder this time, and uncovering the culprit. TOPEKA (1953) starts Elliott off as an outlaw again, but his gang ends up getting rid of a town's rival gang headed by Harry Lauter. Elliott and partner Rick Vallin end up as lawmen, but must then fight their own gang members. Coates and Knight are back in the cast. VIGILANTE TERROR (1953) pits Elliott against masked terrorists headed by Healey. Mary Ellen Kay, a frequent Rex Allen leading lady, shows up here with Knight again. BITTER CREEK (1954) has Elliott, yet again, seeking his brother's killer, Beverly Garland trying to keep him from breaking the law, and Carleton Young as the prominent rancher who, it turns out, is behind it all.

Elliott's last Western movie is THE FORTY-NINERS (1954), in which he plays a marshal assigned to track down three murderers in a California boom town. Veteran badman Lane Bradford plays the sheriff, complete with two pearl-handled guns, but he's still bad, and ends up on the losing side of a gunfight with Elliott's character. Harry Morgan plays a cardsharp who leads Elliott to the killers.

Wild Bill Elliott was no more. But Elliott, simply as Bill Elliott, still had five Allied Artists movies to go in 1955-57. In each of them, he plays a Los Angeles detective; in the first (DIAL RED O) as Lieutenant Flynn and the others as Lieutenant Doyle. SUDDEN DANGER, CALLING HOMICIDE, CHAIN OF EVI-

John Carroll, Bill Elliott, and Catherine McLeod in OLD LOS ANGELES (Republic, 1948).

DENCE, and FOOTSTEPS IN THE NIGHT completed his movie career. He did a TV pilot for a show called "Marshal of Trail City", which reunited him with Dub Taylor, but the series never sold. Neither did "Parson of the West", along the lines of his old HELLFIRE picture.

On a personal level, Elliott's 34-year marriage to Helen Josephine Meyer ended in 1961. His second wife was model Dolly Moore. He moved to Las Vegas where he hosted a weekly TV show interviewing guests and showing one of his old movies. He became an advertising spokesman for a cigarette manufacturer, and died of cancer November 26, 1965.

Elliott's B-Westerns always seemed a cut above the average, from Wild Bill Hickok to Red Ryder, and his A's were tops in practically everyone's Western lists. He perfected the badman-turned-good role pioneered in silent movies by Hart, and was a worthy successor.

BILL ELLIOTT IN THE COMIC BOOKS

Bill Elliott made his first comics appearance in Dell Publishing's Four Color anthology series with #278 (May 1950). The issue features him on the cover in a bright red shirt, gun drawn, and there is a photo back cover as well. For some reason, the title just says 'BILL ELLIOTT'.

As a separate series, WILD BILL ELLIOTT #2 appeared a few months later (November 1950) and ran through #17 (June 1955). Every issue had a photo cover, and numbers 2-10 have photo back covers as well. #2 shows Wild Bill on Thunder, dressed as Red Ryder.

In the midst of this modest run, Wild Bill appeared twice more in the Four Color series, both with photo covers front and back.

Meanwhile, in 1952, Dell's Giant series began a sub-series called *Western Roundup* (the first issue is dated June 1952). The covers featured head photos of Gene Autry and Roy Rogers with smaller shots of Johnny Mack Brown, Rex Allen, and Wild Bill. These were fat comics, with many more pages than ordinary comics (most or all were 84 pages), selling for the high price of 25¢ each.

The first 14 issues had photo back covers, as did #16 and #18. After #18, the photo covers ended, as did the Gene Autry stories. I am not sure how many after that had Wild Bill stories, but by #22 the contents had changed to TV Westerns, such as "Wagon Train" and "Tales of Wells Fargo".

Wild Bill's final appearance was in Four Color #643 (July 1955). Not a bad comic book career for Wild Bill, but not indicative of

his standing as one of the best and most popular movie cowboys.

If Western movie comics had become a staple in the late 1930s
or early 1940s, Wild Bill might have had a much longer comics
career. In those days, as now, superheroes were king. After
the war, a temporary exhaustion of the superhero genre and
increasing adult criticism of the effects of comics on children,
among other factors, led to a greater interest in Westerns. However, for the cowboy series' stars, the interest came a bit late.
Eventually, many Western comics featured TV Westerns, and
ultimately the superheroes came back with a vengeance.

POPULARITY RANKING OF BILL ELLIOTT

The Motion Picture Herald and Box Office Polls were conducted from the mid thirties until the mid 1950s. With few exceptions, the annual results would list the "Top Ten" cowboy film stars. The following are Elliott's rankings in the two Polls.

Year	Motion Picture Herald Poll	Box Office Poll
1938	Not ranked	Not ranked
1939	Not ranked	Not ranked
1940	10th	Not ranked
1941	9th	Not ranked
1942	7th	Not ranked
1943	9th	No poll conducted
1944	5th	Not ranked
1945	4th	5th
1946	2nd	4th
1947	4th	3rd
1948	3rd	4th
1949	5th	4th
1950	4th	5th
1951	6th	8th
1952	4th	5th
1953	4th	9th
1954	4th	Not ranked

In addition to making Westerns, Bill Elliott also enjoyed watching them. In 1954, he listed the following titles for England's *Western Film Annual* as his favorite Westerns. (Titles in no particular order.)

Title	Star
CRIMSON TRAIL	Buck Jones
DYNAMITE RANCH	Ken Maynard
MOONLIGHT ON THE PRAIRIE	Dick Foran
THE LAST ROUNDUP	Gene Autry
TO THE LAST MAN	Randolph Scott
END OF THE TRAIL	Jack Holt
BAR 20 JUSTICE	William Boyd
LAWLESS VALLEY	George O'Brien
TWO GUN LAW	Charles Starrett
PONY POST	Johnny Mack Brown

(Author's Note: Bill Elliott said of one of his favorite pictures: "I've always had a particular soft spot for MOONLIGHT ON THE PRAIRIE, because it gave me my first break in horse operas. No, I wasn't the hero—in fact, I got myself killed halfway through—but I did play the hero's pal and had a chance to get in some good Western action before they polished me off.")

THEY KNEW BILL ELLIOTT

Dorothy Gulliver: Bill Elliott was happy about getting away from Warner Brothers and character parts. He wanted to be a Western star.

Sammy McKim: Bill Elliott was a good rider. I observed him often during the filming of the Hickok serial at the Columbia Ranch and on location at Kanab, Utah. A nice guy and not only did he have a big broad grin with all those good looking teeth of his, but he was a warm person inside. He liked kids, too, and when he knew I collected stamps, he gave a me a lot from his own collection. A warm-hearted guy, a quiet guy, and a great horseman.

Gabby Hayes: Bill Elliott was one fine fellow. I made several pictures with Bill, and we never a had a problem. He was kinda serious, but a friendly man. I think he appreciated my work as much as I appreciated his. I know I had some good parts in Bill's pictures, and he didn't seem to mind at all.

Ben Johnson: Some of my first work in pictures was doubling for Bill Elliott. Bill was a good man, and worked hard at becoming a good horseman; his hard work paid off. I had my first speaking part in one of Bill's pictures. It was only a couple of words, but I was so doggone nervous that I kept flubbing it. After that showing, I'm surprised I ever got as far as I did in the picture business.

Earl Bellamy (director—regarding the making of BEYOND THE SACRAMENTO)**:** The cast worked well together. Bill and Evelyn (Keyes, his feminine lead) were well cast. They enjoyed each other very much. The crew liked them, and happy days and pleasant times were had by all.

Evelyn Keyes: My horse bolted into the hills . . . at the sight of me. Bill Elliott wasn't acting when he lit out to stop that runaway . . . . Personally, I wouldn't trade the experience for anything—horses, guns, and all. It takes all kinds of parts to make a good actress, and I'm sure one of them, for a well-rounded background, is the part I played in BEYOND THE SACRAMENTO.

Lloyd Bridges: I worked with Bill Elliott while I was under contract to Columbia. Bill was kind of a straight-laced man, very, very nice, but he was kind of a loner.

Tris Coffin: Bill Elliott, like Johnny Mack Brown, was one of the nicest, best-liked guys in the business. Everyone enjoyed working in Bill's and Johnny's pictures. The same cannot be said about Allan Lane. I worked with Bill and Allan when they were doing the "Red Ryder" pictures, and with Allan in his Rocky Lane series. And I will tell you it was no fun working with Allan. If you were doing a movie, and it was not a Rocky Lane film, and you loused up a line or a scene, invariably, the director or somebody would say, "The next time that happens, you go into a Rocky Lane picture." I guess Allan meant well, but he had an unfortunate personality. He was nothing like Bill Elliott.

(Author's note: Coffin's memory did not serve him well. He worked only in one Rocky Lane feature, but none of the "Red Ryder" Westerns.)

Jimmy Wakely: While in Big Spring, Texas, Bill Elliott and I roomed together. One day, he got a call from his agent telling him that Herb Yates wanted to take him out of the "Red Ryder" pictures, and make an even bigger star of him—make him big in "legit" features. Bill was scared. He told me how good he was doing, how much money he had in the bank, how broke he used to be, and how grateful he was to be where he was. He said, "My God, Jimmy, I just don't know about leaving the Red Ryders." The next morning, we were in a hotel room in a small town called Mineral Wells. Elliott was staring out the window at a movie theater below. The marquee advertised Bill Elliott as Red Ryder, and there was a line of kids a block and a half long. "This is why I hate to leave the Red Ryders," Elliott said, pointing to the kids below, "because that's where they are. They love me, and they will always be my fans. If I leave it . . . well, it scares me to death." The studio put him into some big features anyway, but he didn't click like they thought. And I hurt for him. I know he was very proud of being Red Ryder.

Joe Kane (director): One day, Wild Bill called me aside on the set and really lit into me. I could not believe what he was saying. He told me that if I thought I was doing him a favor getting him to do this picture (IN OLD SACRAMENTO) rather than Randy Scott, I should forget it! He had been perfectly content playing Red Ryder. What the devil could I say? Later on, he changed his mind. Other than that one time, I never had any problems with Wild Bill.

Roy Barcroft: He (Bill Elliott) wanted to get into big features which was a mistake for him. Suddenly, he thought he was leading-man material; he wanted to be a romantic lead, and Republic was looking for a leading man for Vera Ralston. She was the girlfriend of Herbert J. Yates, the man who owned Republic Studios. He couldn't get anybody to work with her; she was that bad. And he was going to make a star out of her or else. She was a skater originally—very beautiful, but as an actress, she couldn't cut it. And she had a terrific accent anyway; she was Czechoslovakian. So he got Bill Elliott and said, "We'll move you up, and make you her leading man." Well, he was tickled to death to do it, and he made one feature with her as her leading man and the next one, he comes back and does her father. This just upset him to no end. So then Bill just cut out of the studio all together, and produced a couple of shows on his own; he didn't make any money, and it broke him. He borrowed money to do it. He never knew he had cancer. He was living in Las Vegas when he died. I had just visited him the week before, and when I suggested we go out for a drink, he advised he didn't feel well. A few days later, he was gone. We made several "Red Ryder" films together. I always liked working with Wild Bill; he was a man of ethics. Towards the end of his career, he was making a great deal of money doing cigarette commercials. Strange, but he often told me that it bothered him pushing the sale of tobacco; he felt that he was letting down his fans and their children as well.

Tex Ritter (regarding being teamed with Elliott): Elliott was frank about it, as I suppose I was too. Bill was a gentleman and a very fine actor. I admired and respected him very much. He hadn't started off in pictures starring in Westerns as Autry and I had. Bill had played various kinds of roles and bit parts for years before they put him in cowboy duds. Of course, Columbia gave us all kinds of excuses for teaming us up—the Three Mesquiteers over at Republic were doing well, and, the teaming of stars was inevitable. Of course, we'd rather it happened to somebody else and not us, but . . . anyway Columbia was aware that they would have to use more music in their movies because of the success of Autry and Rogers. They had Charlie Starrett who didn't sing, so they brought in the Sons of the Pioneers. Elliott didn't sing either, so they had to have somebody, and that's where I came in, I suppose. Right away, Bill called me aside, and informed me that there was nothing personal about it, but wanted me to know that he wasn't too keen on the idea, and that he was keeping an eye open for any situation whereby he could solo again. I felt that was being open and frank, and I admired the way he laid it on me. I, also, told him my feelings were about the same. Unfortunately for me, after that series was over, he landed what he wanted at Republic, while I had to do it all over again with Johnny Mack Brown at Universal. I really enjoyed working with him (Elliott), and he was a very likeable fellow. He rode like he was born in the saddle, although like me (and he laughed), he had a double for any dangerous stunts. He was the star, but I think we had equal time to show what we could do. I guess you have to call it a fifty-fifty set-up, and we got along just fine.

Frank Mitchell: I replaced Dub Taylor in the Elliottt/Ritter series. Dub had been called Cannonball, so the studio just decided to call me Cannonball too. Bill and Tex were wonderful guys to work with. There was no jealousy between them, but I'm sure they would have been happier having their own series.

John Duncan: When I was growing up back in Missouri, my dad had a barber shop next door to a drugstore. I used to buy cherry-phosphate sodas there, and the soda-jerk was Bill Elliott. One day, he came by all dressed up, and told us he was going to Hollywood and try to become a motion picture actor. Some years later, I was making a film on the lot next to where Bill was shooting. I went over and introduced myself as the kid who liked cherry-phosphate sodas. We had a good laugh about that.

(Author's Note: In addition to his other films, John Duncan played Robin in the 1949 Columbia serial, BATMAN AND ROBIN.)

Marie Windsor: Bill Elliott saw the test I'd made as well as the George Raft film (OUTPOST IN MOROCCO), and when he learned I was a horsewoman, he fought the studio to use me

(HELLFIRE) instead of one of their contract players. He later taught me how to twirl guns, and I did a lot of stuntwork in this Western that normally an actress simply would not do. Bill had a high academic and rather "socially best school" background. He couldn't hide that quality whatever his Western garb might be. I always of thought Bill as "the" Western gentleman cowboy. Bill's personality was about the same, on camera or off, with his voice and mannerism. HELLFIRE should have been a Western that would have changed my whole career. Studio owner Herbert Yates promised to spend a lot of money to sell the film. Mr. Yates suddenly got involved in trying to get the communists out of the industry. He made a film called THE RED MENACE, which he spent a great amount of money to sell and did nothing for HELLFIRE.

Peggy Stewart: When Don Barry and I divorced, he talked to Herbert Yates (Republic studio head). They were starting the "Red Ryder" series. Bill Elliott was going to be doing it. Don told Yates that I was a good rider and could act, and asked him to give me a chance in the picture. So they put me in TUCSON RAIDERS. I'm sure Don got me a contract so he wouldn't have to pay alimony.

Jim Bannon: I was the last Red Ryder. I knew two of the other three who played Ryder, Bill Elliott and Rocky Lane. I saw Don Barry around Hollywood a few times, but never knew him. Barry played Ryder first—in a serial. I knew the other two fairly well. Bill Elliott was an alright guy, real easy-going, and everyone had a lot of respect for him as person and as a movie cowboy. Lane didn't have any friends; he was too damn conceited; he was too stuck on himself.

Tom London: I made a lot of pictures with a lot of cowboy stars. I especially liked working with Bill Elliott. He knew his business, and everyone was treated nice on his pictures.

Rex Allen: Bill had a 60-acre ranch right out of Woodland Hills, and I used to go visit him. He had the greatest spur collection I have ever seen in my life. Bill Elliott was a guy you had to admire because he was not a cowboy when he started. He was a male model from New York. This man really became a top horseman. Bill was a cowboy, and I mean a good one. He worked a lot with Glenn Randall (horse trainer). When I started out, I wanted to be different. I did not want people saying I was copying Roy or Gene or some of the other Western stars, so I decided I'd wear my guns turned around backwards. I didn't know for two years that Bill Elliott did it too.

Pierce Lyden: Although I worked in motion pictures with a great many stars, there were only a few I ever got to know well. One cowboy star who became my friend was Wild Bill Elliott, a man respected by everyone who knew him. Bill was polite and sociable, but soft-spoken. We met during the filming of KING OF DODGE CITY, in which he starred with Tex Ritter. Bill took dramatic lessons, something most Western stars paid little attention to. Of the few Western stars who were good actors, Bill was right up there at the top. Once, during a chase, my horse stumbled, and we hit the ground. Bill stopped the chase, and was the first one back to check on me. I was hurt, but on a low-budget picture an injury to a supporting actor didn't always mean much. Elliott stuck his neck out for me. "We'll do the scene later," he said. When I was well, we did a retake, but I don't think he got paid for it. People were more important than money to Wild Bill. Having decided to follow in the footsteps of his idol, cowboy star William S. Hart, he bought guns, belts, and all kinds of Western gear. Then he spent hour on hour learning to ride and twirl guns, establishing his own identity with the famous two six-shooters reversed. He had a unique riding style, which he taught me—a dignified style, easily recognized by Western fans. I guess what made Bill spend so much time with me was that he considered me sober and dedicated, trying seriously for the "brass ring" of fame he had already grabbed. Another skill he taught me was to put a razor blade in a piece of wood, and use it to cut two- or three-inch strips out of rawhide for thongs and laces. We used them to tie our blankets or raincoats down behind our saddle. Sometime later, Herbert Yates, head of Republic, decided to change Bill's name to William and reshape his image. I was sorry to hear it. Yates was taking away a name kids could remember and relate to. He also took away the action—and Bill loved action. Unfortunately, because Western pictures were on the downhill pull, the build-up didn't work. We made a lot of films together—had a lot of fun. Wild Bill Elliott was one of a kind.

Dub Taylor: All the Western stars I worked with were great cowboys—Wild Bill Elliott, Charlie Starrett, and Russell Hayden. I especially liked working with Wild Bill Elliott. I thought we made a good team. Wild Bill was a good fellow and real nice to me.

(Author's Note: Taylor did not mention Jimmy Wakely with whom he made several movies.)

Adele Mara: Bill Elliott was a very stiff person. Very rigid. When he walked from here to there, he never budged from one side to the other. I never had any conversation with him at all.

Anne Jeffreys: Working with Bill Elliott was wonderful. I even got to sing a couple of songs. Gabby Hayes was a darling man. Bill was originally a dress extra, and somebody talked him into doing the "Red Ryder" series—probably Pappy Yates, who ran Republic. He was very tall—6' 3 or 6' 4, and of course, he had those boots, making him a giant. He was a man who knew what he wanted, smart businesswise. Everything was very well calculated and worked out in his career. He had it all planned—what he was going to do and how he was going to do it. And he accomplished it. He became a big Western star practically overnight. He was always reserved and quiet, but fun . . . had a nice sense of humor.

(Author's Note: According to published sources, in his prime, Elliott stood 6' 1 and weighed 173.)

Adrian Booth: He was very professional. He really loved his work. He was very good . . . very easy to work with, but he was a bit wooden.

Barbra Fuller: I liked Bill Elliott. He was very helpful. He was a little on the wolfish side, but I didn't have any trouble with him. One time, when I had to ride up to the camera and do a quick dismount, the wardrobe woman, afterwards, said to me, "Did you notice Mr. Elliott . . . he was standing right behind the camera, ready to grab the horse if you had any problems." So he was caring, and I knew very little about Western riding.

Spencer Gordon Bennet (director): Bill Elliott admired Buck Jones, and tried to fashion his screen work after him. This was true when he started at Columbia and still true when he joined Republic.

(Author's Note: Most people said Elliott tried to fashion himself after William S. Hart.)

Linda Stirling: I was very fond of Bill. He was so courteous and gentle. Here's this tall, very good looking hunk, but he was sweet and very caring about everybody else, making sure we were all comfortable in a scene. I don't remember him ever raising his voice. He was always gentle, quiet, and ready to go with a scene. He was kind and a gentleman, but serious about being a good cowboy.

Bobby Blake: The makeup room at the studio (Republic) was a particularly unique and lovely place that I got to be part of. The cowboys didn't go to the makeup room. They got their makeup down on the set. I guess Bill Elliott may have gone in there to get his hairpiece on. Now Bill Elliott was easy to get along with because he was a sweet, very gentle, wonderful man. I mean Red Ryder always said he was a peaceable man, and Bill Elliott truly was peaceable. Allan Lane. on the other hand . . . .

(Author's Note: I stopped here with Blake's comments because I do not wish to see language like he used in describing Lane in my work.)

John Pickard: Wild Bill Elliott, who was a dress actor, made himself into a tremendous cowboy. He decided he wanted to be a Western star; and he was one of the best. He was a two-gun man. I made pictures with Bill, and I was the heavy in most of them. So Bill and I had a scene when I come around the corner of a barn, and he comes around the other corner; he's going to draw on me and cut me down, because I'm a bad guy. Well, I beat him to the draw in this particular case; he didn't like that, because he was a very fast two-gun man. It was kind of a funny story on the set for awhile.

Tom Steele: I doubled Bill Elliott and Allan Lane in all the "Red Ryder" pictures, then I doubled Lane in the Rocky Lane series. My physique and facial structure was so similar to theirs that it is virtually impossible for anyone to tell it's me doubling them. Bill was nice to work with; Lane was a pain in the neck.

Mary Ellen Kay: Bill Elliott was sort of like a father to me. Being away from home, I felt he brought out some daughter-like feelings in me. I remember we were out on location, and he said, "I just want you to know that we (Elliott and the other cowboys) are going on a tough ride for this next scene." He didn't think I could handle it, and might want a stuntwoman to take my place. But I piped up, "I can do that." So off we went without a rehearsal among the mountains and rocks, going faster and faster. I'm thinking, "This is fun. I'm having a good time." Suddenly, the shot is over, and everybody reins in their horses—except me. I couldn't get my horse to stop running. I yelled out, "Loose horse! Loose horse!" And pretty soon, out of the corner of my eye, I could see a rider coming after me—it was Bill. He rode up beside me, grabbed my reins, and stopped my horse the exact same way any good hero would do.

Marshall Reed: When Bill Elliott found out he was getting promoted to bigger pictures, he went to Herb Yates, and put in a good word for me to take over his Red Ryder role. Yates agreed, but later changed his mind and gave it to Rocky Lane. I always had a lot of respect for Bill Elliott. He was one of the nicer guys in the picture business.

Sunset Carson: I worked with Bill Elliott when several of us cowboys appeared in the Roy Rogers movie BELLS OF ROSARITA. Bill was a good guy and a great cowboy star. Somebody once told me Bill got $2,000 for that picture. If he did, that's more than all the rest of us got.

Terry Frost: Most of the cowboy stars were good guys. Bill Elliott was one. He cared about the people who were working with him. Some of the other guys were no-class, but I wouldn't take any of their stuff because I had been around, and knew how to take care of myself.

R. G. Springsteen (director): I worked on several of the Red Ryder pictures with both Bill Elliott and Allan Lane. I had much rather talk about Bill Elliott. I don't think he ever gave any of the directors any trouble . . . the way that Lane sometimes did. All the people on the set liked Bill.

Phyllis Coates: Bill Elliott looked and acted very much like the cowboy hero—very macho. He was somewhat quiet and serious, but a very likeable man. He was tall, straight, and nice looking. Unlike myself, who could barely ride, Bill was a superb horseman. He really made an excellent Western star. Probably the best cowboy, even better than some guys I worked with who were bigger names and better looking, was Wild Bill Elliott. He was the best cowboy.

Constance Moore: Making IN OLD SACRAMENTO was a lot of fun to do. Bill was so nice, a real gentleman. The thing that comes to mind most about the movie is the premiere. We went up to Sacramento in a chartered plane. Bill and I did a couple of personal appearances, a parade, a radio show, and went to the theater for the premiere.

Bob Brown (leather crafter for many of the Western stars): Bill was selected as Sheriff Gene Biscalagi's rodeo field general in 1948 at the Los Angeles Coliseum. They came to me to donate a trophy for the best Western working cowboy contest. I was in business on Hollywood Boulevard at the time. It just happened that Bill Elliott won all-around best looking working cowboy horse and equipment. He won my leather carved plaque that day.

Johnny Western: I was under consideration for a proposed TV Western, so I decided I needed a good-looking horse. I wanted one with a blaze face and four white stockings. I inquired around and was told that Bill Elliott had such a horse. I was given Elliott's telephone number and contacted him. He told me I could see the horse at the stable and then call him at home if I was still interested. The horse was just what I was looking for, so I called Bill to get directions to his house. When I got there, I knocked and heard Bill's voice telling me to come in. To my surprise, he was up on a ladder in full painters' gear (including the hat), painting the room. he told me he had promised his wife that he would get the painting completed that day and told me just to look around for a little while until he got through. After about 15 minutes, Bill came out and we discussed the horse. I was afraid I couldn't afford it, and I was right. But, after seeing a star like Bill Elliott on that ladder, I learned one thing—star or no star—we all have to put our pants on one leg at a time, and we all have our little chores to do.

Harry Carey, Jr.: I met Bill Elliott twice. The first time was in 1939 at a rodeo. They had a horse race featuring several movie cowboys including Bill, Big Boy Williams, and Tex Ritter. Bill won the race. It was funny because when the race was over, Tex couldn't stop his horse and it ran right out of the arena, and he never rode back in. The second time I saw Bill was when Pat Ford, John Ford's son, and I went out to his place to ride with him. Bill had some fine horses. Bill Elliott was a friendly fellow, really wonderful and down to earth. He worked hard at becoming a cowboy, and he really made good at it.

(Author's Note: Tex Ritter's problem with his horse, White Flash, at the rodeo was not an isolated incident. While making a picture with Johnny Mack Brown, Tex was unable to rein in the horse and it ran over Jimmy Wakely. It sent Wakely sprawling, tore his shirt, and gave him several bumps and bruises. John Hall also wrote in Wrangler's Roost of incidents involving Tex and White Flash: Old Tex McCleod's son, Clyde, was Johnny Mack Brown's double in the Brown/Ritter series, and sometimes doubled Tex Ritter as well. He told me: "White Flash was an awkward, big horse. On the first day's shooting Tex had to ride into town and, while coming down the main street, Flash threw him off. They did it again with Forrest Burns dressed as Ritter and it happened again. Only this time, Flash rode straight into a wagon and Forrest caught his foot in one of the wheels. He broke his ankle, and was never able to walk properly again." Clyde explained how bad the horse was and that they mostly used other white horses as doubles. Dorothy Fay, Tex's wife, also recalled just how bad the horse was: "It was a very wild stallion and Tex had to have him gelded, so they used a double called Nevada.")

BILL ELLIOTT AND HIS HORSES

He was always well-mounted, on-screen and off. In his early Columbia pictures, he rode a studio-rented horse called Dice, but quickly abandoned him in favor of his own mount, a handsome paint named Sonny. Bill and Sonny were constant companions throughout his early career and on into his association with Republic studios. Bill switched to another horse for his "Red Ryder" series: this was the magnificent black stallion, Thunder. Elliott rode Thunder for two years.

For the upgraded Republic pictures, he purchased a handsome, gray, quarter horse stud named Stormy Day Moore from the Waggoner estate in Texas. Stormy was one of the best looking horses to ever enjoy a screen career, and was just perfect in size and conformation for Bill's lanky form.

Away from the camera, Bill was a real-life cowboy and rancher, raising not only herefords and quarter horses, but being an enthusiastic cutting-horse fan as well.

Records show that, in 1950, Bill Elliott purchased a good cutting horse called Red Boy from Lloyd Jenkins of Fort Worth, Texas. The horse carried the National Cutting Horse Association certificate of ability No. 47 and was registered under the AQHA No. 15810, which would identify him as Rey Boy (apparently Elliott had changed the horse's name) sired by Billy by King P-234, out of a Swenson ranch mare (Niwad). Bill campaigned Red Boy successfully until he sold the horse in 1956.

The gelding went on to earn, in his lifetime, $20,000.00 in MCHA approved shows. Elliott was also a member of the National Cutting Horse Association, and in 1952 served on the executive committee. (*Horse and Rider* article by Lewis Smith.)

Elliott rode a pinto named Dice in some of his Columbia seri-

Bill Elliott and horse, Sonny, showing off.

als. A similar pinto called Sonny became Bill's mount in his Columbia, and his early Republic features. *(William Elliott and Robert Livingston "The Knights of the Range" by Mario DeMarco).*

(Author's Note: Dice was a studio rental mount, and appeared in many films with various riders throughout the years. The horse is easily distinguishable from Sonny due to its solid white face. It was a pinto stallion with flashy coloring and a repertoire of tricks usable in Westerns. The horse was also ridden by Jean Arthur in ARIZONA (1940, Columbia), and it was featured in DUEL IN THE SUN (1947, Selznick). It last appeared in THUNDERHOOF (1948, Columbia).

A Wild Bill Elliott comic book made it to the stands in 1950. Published quarterly by Dell, the comic had Wild Bill riding a black stallion named Stormy through 20 issues. (*Those Six-Gun Heroes* by Douglas E. Nye.)

Wild Bill Elliott purchased the Morgan, Andy Pershing 8390, from its breeder C. G. Stevenson. He was the horse Thunder in the "Red Ryder" movies. (*The Morgan Horse*, February 1945, page 27.)

Andy Pershing 8390 (Thunder) was bred by C. G. Stevenson of Des Moines, Iowa and foaled in 1940. His sire was General Pershing, and his dam was Ann Bartlett . . . Andy was the sire of eleven Morgans who were foaled from 1943 to 1957. The Morgan horse register Volume VI shows Andy Pershing had transfers to the following owners: C. G. Stevenson, C. G. And Beatrice Stevenson, Horseshoe Cattle Co. (1941), Mrs. Anne K. Zeitler (1942), Berman Stock Farm, Inc. (1943), Bill Elliott (1943), and Allan Lane (1946). *(Morgan Horse Directory—Northern California Club,* 1969, p. 3.)

(Rex Allen): A lot of people don't know it, but Rocky Lane bought Black Jack from Bill Elliott—the horse he rode in the "Red Ryder" series. Bill owned the world champion cutting horse. His name was Red Man.

(Bill Elliott): I'd like to tell you about Thunder, and I don't mean the thunder that rumbles in the sky, but the black horse I have ridden in all the "Red Ryder" Westerns. It was quite a job to find a horse to play the role of Thunder because a horse is very important in a motion picture. A cowboy thinks a lot of his horse, and asks a lot of him. The horse must have a nice quiet, disposition, must be able to run at a tremendous speed, and when you bring him into a close-up, he must remain quiet so that he will not interfere with dialogue. After looking at 40 or 50

Bill Elliott , shown as he rode out in to the Los Angeles Coliseum on his beautiful black horse, Thunder at a rally for Thomas Dewey.

black horses, I finally selected this one which I now own and call Thunder.

At every rodeo performance, I will be in the arena riding Thunder, and will show him in a series of his tricks. He dances, goes to the mailbox, and gets the mail for me, pushes a baby buggy, picks my hat off the ground, and hands it up to me, sits down, and I put on his glasses while he holds the funny paper in his mouth and reads it. He also says his prayers and I think

Bill Elliott practices his rope spinning on his personal horse, "Stormy Night." The two were between scenes on THE FABULOUS TEXAN. (Republic, 1947).

that it is very important that boys and girls say their prayers, and that goes for us grown-ups, too.

Thunder is a very beautiful horse in my opinion. He stands 15-1/2 hands and weighs 1,150 pounds. I bought him from Levi Garrett, of Sterling City, Texas. Thunder has traveled with me all over the United States.

In my spare time between pictures, I often take Thunder to the children's hospitals and entertain the boys and girls who can't get out and run and play and ride like well children can. When I take Thunder into the hospital wards, I don't even have a halter on him. He walks in and around all the kiddies, and he is just as careful as can be. Lots of times, I let the boys and girls ride him. I have had as many as six children on his back at once.

I think Thunder is just about the finest horse any cowboy could ever hope to own. I am very careful in what I feed him. I never give him sugar because I don't think it is good for him. He prefers carrots. They keep his hair nice and shiny, and make his diet balanced. He gets a combination of hay every day, with a flake of alfalfa for breakfast and a flake of oat hay for his dinner. I have a special mixture of grain that I give him at every meal.

I have a special horse trailer in which I carry both Thunder and Stormy Night, my quarter horse stallion, which I also will ride in every rodeo performance. Stormy and Thunder are always kept stabled next to each other as they are very good friends, and anytime I have ever separated them, I am sure they missed one another.

There's lots more things I'd like to tell you about Thunder and Stormy, but I'd rather you'd see them yourself. I always like to talk about these two horses, so I hope the opportunity comes up soon for me to tell you some more.

THEY'RE TALKING ABOUT BILL ELLIOTT

How young Gordon (Bill Elliott) Nance came to deciding on an acting career is quite interesting indeed. It was said that his mother once made a visit to a fortune teller, and to her surprise, the prophet predicted that her son would one day become a famous movie actor. Gordon carried this fact in his mind for a number of years before actually pursuing it. (*William Elliott and Robert Livingston "The Knights of the Range"* by Mario DeMarco.)

OVERLAND WITH KIT CARSON proved very popular with kids, including television's Johnny Carson, who was living in Norfolk, Nebraska at the time. "That serial was very important to me," Carson recalled during his beautifully nostalgic TV special "Johnny Goes Marching Home" in 1982. Such a comment is a perfect example of the high place Westerns held in the hearts of many kids of the 1930s and 1940s. (*Those Six-Gun Heroes* by Douglas E. Nye.)

(Regarding Elliott's serials): Columbia had few stars of any real magnitude. William Elliott was the most popular, appearing in THE GREAT ADVENTURES OF WILD BILL HICKOK, OVERLAND WITH KIT CARSON, and THE VALLEY OF VANISHING MEN. Elliott was an exceptionally appealing performer, excelling both in dialogue delivery and action sequences, and he became one of Columbia's better all-around Western heroes. When he moved over to Republic, again to receive high popular acceptance, he made no serial appearances, and many of his fans felt shortchanged. (*Saturday Afternoon at the Movies* by Alan Barbour.)

(Author's Note: When Elliott signed with Republic, he asked to be excluded from serials.)

Bill Elliott's 10th starring B-Western for Columbia Pictures and his fourth outing as frontier tamer Wild Bill Hickok (including the 1938 serial THE GREAT ADVENTURES OF WILD BILL HICKOK), BEYOND THE SACRAMENTO (working title: GHOST GUNS) confines 95% of its screening to sound stage interiors' lensing and shots on the studio's Western town set. This oater was the solo entry into the B-Western genre for rising dramatic actress Evelyn Keyes, fresh from her plum role as one of Vivien Leigh's sisters, in Metro-Goldwyn-Mayer's soon-to-be-famous Civil War screen classic, GONE WITH THE WIND (1939) . . . She (Keyes) personally elevates an otherwise routine role. (*Under Western Skies* article by Richard B. Smith III.)

In 1941, Columbia Pictures teamed two popular Western stars (Bill Elliott and Tex Ritter) in one of their most successful series. Bill Elliott had become the studio's second favorite star, next to Charles Starrett . . . Tex Ritter had done two successful series for Ed Finney Productions at Grand National, and Monogram, but when he came to Columbia he had to take second billing to Elliott . . . Elliott and Ritter made an interesting team. Elliott was a big and handsome man who looked every inch like a hero. His fists were formidable weapons, as screen villains quickly learned, but there was also an affable side to Elliott that the girls found charming, especially when he flashed that winning smile. Ritter lacked Elliott's rugged physical presence, but his talent with a tune made him extremely popular. As a singing cowboy, who for a time rivaled Gene Autry, he was billed as "America's Most Beloved Cowboy." (*Classic Images* article by Mike Newton.)

After signing Tex (Ritter), Columbia was determined to com-
bine the singing cowboy concept with the trio. Elliott no more
wanted to be relegated to co-star status than did Ritter, but
Wild Bill and the amiable Tex remained friendly, even though
on screen Tex became the less important of the two. The formula called for Tex and Wild Bill to conflict with each other
throughout most of the film, before combining at last to thwart
the villains. For 1942, Elliott rose to seventh among Top Ten
Western Stars, his highest finish to date. Apparently, co-starring with Tex Ritter boosted Elliott's career, but he had no in-
tention of continuing to share Columbia's screen. For 1943,
Elliott left Columbia for Republic, the best in the business at
making B-Westerns. (*Tex Ritter, America's Most Beloved Cowboy* by Bill O'Neal.)

Wild Bill made a total of 24 sagebrush sagas at Columbia,
then rode his horse to the widening corral at Republic. After
his arrival at Republic, it was the closest a B-Western cowpoke could get to heaven without dying, and had it happened
earlier, he might have given Republic's top hands, Gene and
Roy, some competition for all their fancy titles . . . The studio
launched a massive campaign to move him (Roy) into Autry's
former no. 1 position on the totem pole. Roy shot upward in
popularity as if he'd been fired from a rocket. Wild Bill settled
into his cowboy self-persona, and went about making good
pictures and holding his own. (*The Old Cowboy Picture Show*
article by Robert W. Phillips.)

(Regarding a movie ad for ROLL ALONG COWBOY (a Smith
Ballew starring picture, where Wild Bill Elliott is listed in bold
letters across the ad—Elliott wore a mustache and was a villain in the film): When this movie was first released there was
nothing about Wild Bill Elliott in the advertisements. After Elliott
became one of the more popular Western stars, then some-

one decided to cash in on his name, and the name Wild Bill Elliott was added to the advertisement when the movie was re-released. This must have caused some conternation among Elliott's fans as they watched Wild Bill get worked over by some tall drink of water that spent a lot of time singing. The people who released the movie again could have cared less. The photo does not say starring Wild Bill Elliott, but even the small kids knew that the first name, and the name in the largest print was the star of the movie, Sorry, not this time. (*Classic Images* article by Don Creacy.)

Like Tom Mix, Bill liked to have young children cast in his films. He insisted the scenarist write a youngster in at some point. Only when he got to Republic could Bill wield enough influence to have youngsters given speaking parts of a more substantial nature, and, once he was playing Red Ryder, he was delighted at having young Bobby Blake as his partner. The love of children offset the customary severity of Bill's characterization. (*The Filming of the West* by Jon Tuska.)

HIDDEN VALLEY OUTLAWS (working title: THE OUTLAW BUSTER) was Wild Bill Elliott's 32nd starring B-Western and his eighth for Republic Pictures. He would take a two-and-a-half month respite from appearing before the cameras until TUCSON RAIDERS (1944), his initial entry in the studio's soon-to-be famous "Red Ryder" series. Elliott would film 16 of those oatburners into the fall of 1945. (*Under Western Skies* article by Richard B. Smith III.)

Bill Elliott was excluded (when signed by Republic) from appearing in serials and allowed to furnish his own mounts . . . for which Republic paid him the going rate charged by rental stables for stock steeds . . . he entered into a one year term contract for eight Westerns at $2750 each . . . Elliott was paid $2000 for a cameo in Roy Rogers' BELLS OF ROSARITA (1945), and waived his top-billing clause on the condition of being credited first of the other cowboy guest stars . . . . Elliott took on the title role in the first 16 entries (Red Ryder) under two successive term-picture contracts calling for eight pictures in the first year at $3750 each, then eight more the second year at $4750 each. (*Republic Confidential —Volume 2, The Players* by Jack Mathis.)

During the run of the Ryder series, he had guest starred in Roy Rogers' BELLS OF ROSARITA with some other Republic favorites, Allan Lane, Bob Livingston, Sunset Carson, and Don Barry. Also in the cast was young Barbara Elliott, Bill's daughter by his then wife, Helen. (*Wrangler's Roost* article by John Hall.)

Gabby (Hayes) had done his job well in the (Roy) Rogers series, which was second only to Autry's. Herbert Yates, the head of the studio (Republic), felt Gabby could do much to help build the new Bill Elliott series into a winner, and that Smiley (Burnette) should move to the Rogers series where in years past he had proven his ability to work with Rogers. (*Those Great Cowboy Sidekicks* by David Rothel.)

In 1944, Republic brought Red Ryder back to the silver screen (some four years after the Red Ryder serial featuring Don Barry) in TUCSON RAIDERS, the first in a series of 16 feature-length films starring William "Wild Bill" Elliott, a veteran of Western serials and features. Elliott incorporated some of his personal trademarks, including his twin, reverse-holstered, bone-handled revolvers and his "I'm a peaceable man, but . . ." introduction to slam-bang action, into his Red Ryder characterization. Yet, to many fans, Elliott remains the favorite movie Red Ryder. Bowing out of the Ryder series in 1946 with CONQUEST OF CHEYENNE . . . In a moving speech at the Golden Boot Awards dinner in 1984, Robert Blake acknowledged his earlier repudiation of the Little Beaver role, attributing his previous attitude to a deep-seated, private denial of his years as a child actor. To the delight of fans who have enjoyed his rise from child star to seasoned adult performer, Blake took this occasion to recant his earlier disdain for the role of Little Beaver. He announced his acceptance of the characterization as well as pride in his association with Western films in general. While other boys his age could only sit in theaters and enjoy vicariously the adventures of Red Ryder and other Western stars, he had been fortunate enough to have been there. (*Under Western Skies* article by Jim Ryan.)

Elliott was a serious student of the West. His movie idol was the legendary silent Western great William S. Hart, who was considered the greatest in his field. Bill personally knew Hart, and would visit the then retired star at his beautiful and spacious "working" ranch at Newhall. Here, both stars would discuss the West and making Western films. (*William Elliott and Robert Livingston "The Knights of the Range"* by Mario DeMarco.)

A *Wild Bill Elliott* comic book made it to the stands in 1950. Published quarterly by Dell, the comic had Wild Bill riding a black stallion named Stormy through 20 issues. *(Those Six-Gun Heroes* by Douglas E. Nye.)

Having built Bill Elliott into a top Western star via a series of expert and fast-moving "B"s, they (Republic) changed Bill to William, and promoted him to nine-reel historical Western "specials", in which he was tied down by frock coats and silk shirts, reels of dialogue, studio "exteriors", and back projection, and far too little fresh air, horses, and wagons. Expensive films like IN OLD SACRAMENTO and PLAINSMAN AND THE LADY contained a quarter of the action or appeal of his five-reelers, and he lost much of his popularity until he reverted to his former style—and scale— with a good "B" series at Monogram. (*A Pictorial History of the Western Film* by William K. Everson.)

(Regarding Elliott's Republic big-budget Westerns): Unfortunately, Bill was often saddled with Republic president Herbert J. Yates' girlfriend (later wife) wanna-be star, Vera Ralston. Her miscasting often harmed otherwise good films. There is a marked difference when Marie Windsor was Elliott's leading lady. *(Top 100 Cowboys of the Century* by Boyd Magers.)

(Author's Note: In his rating of the top 100 cowboys, Magers listed Elliott at number 18.)

After completing the last one in the William Elliott (high-budget Westerns) series, THE SHOWDOWN, Bill left Republic, and signed to do a series for Monogram Pictures, later to become Allied Artists Pictures. Although the Monogram/Allied Artists series didn't have the polish and budgets behind them of the Republic productions, they did have good scripts and a realistic approach. Starting with THE LONGHORN, Bill made 11 in this series . . . Bill then did five detective features for Allied Artists. Although not as good as his Westerns, Bill didn't do too badly with this series, and it was entertaining. So with FOOTSTEPS IN THE NIGHT, released in 1957, Bill's movie career ended, having started back in 1925. *(Wild Bill Elliott* by John W. Leonard.)

Wild Bill was easy to work with, and his fellow actors became his close friends. One of the closest being Roy Barcroft, the villain of hundreds of Western films. Their friendship had ripened over a period of 18 years, despite Barcroft's nasty habit of hiding Bill's toupee. Yes, he did wear one, many of them did. *(Horse & Rider* article by Lewis Smith.)

Monogram, in the process of changing itself into Allied Artists and concentrating on a higher-bracket product, also started an intelligent new series with Bill Elliott. While Ellliott remained essentially a man of intergrity, at the same time, he upset many of the Boy Scout behavior codes by which most of the cowboy heroes had abided since Tom Mix's day. *(A Pictorial History of the Western Film* by William K. Everson.)

It was his last series of Westerns (Allied Artists) that has prompted film historians to compare Wild Bill to William S. Hart. Elliott did act in a more realistic, adult manner, drinking and smoking when it seemed the natural thing to do. And he was not above taking unfair advantage of an enemy, holding him at gunpoint while he beat the daylights out of him. (*Those Six-Gun Heroes* by Douglas E. Nye.)

Monogram Pictures, during January 1952, was charged in a $225,000 damage suit with luring Bill Elliott to the studio. The legal action, filed by Century Television Productions, claimed Elliott previously signed with the TV outfit in June 1950 and had appeared in a pilot film "Marshal of Trail City" which was shown to Monogram officials. The suit further charged that the cowboy star, by contracting to a Monogram movie pact, ignored the original Century tie-up. (*Western Clippings* article by Richard B. Smith III.)

"Marshal of Trail City", filmed in 1950 by Century Television Productions, was another pilot starring "Wild" Bill Elliott which never developed into a series for reasons unknown. Elliott portrayed his movie image "I'm a peaceable man" philosophy who becomes the marshal of Trail City, a town near his ranch. Trail City is the end of a long trail for Texas cattle herds and a town made up of trail drivers, gunhands, and other restless souls who have never learned to respect any law except that of a blazing six-gun . . . . In 1957, Elliott filmed another pilot for a possible television series entitled "El Coyote" It too was shot down. (*Classic TV Westerns* by Ronald Jackson.)

In 1957, he called it quits. He sold his engraved six-guns to Tommy L. Bish, then a *Gun World* staffer, and retired to his ranch in Las Vegas, where he began to dabble in real estate and land development . . . it was in the early sixties that he came back to Hollywood long enough to do a commercial for a cigarette company (Viceroy). (*Gun World* article by Jack Lewis.)

(Author's Note: These were not the same guns that were on display at a Las Vegas restaurant at the time of Elliott's death.)

The cool cowboy star chalked a distinguished record for three companies and an assortment of roles, including leads in some medium to high-budgeted productions. Behind them all was that steely, reassuring calm. You wanted him on you side . . . . His Westerns were, in general, uncommonly good. Sometimes, he would be better than his material; frequently, he alone would hold a shaky vehicle together. He always projected integrity, and a placid, rather remote nobility. He was once quoted as saying he wanted to portray Williams S. Hart in a screen biography. He didn't much resemble Hart physically, but he might well have patterned his style after the great silent star. It would have been good casting. (*Hollywood Corral* by Don Miller.)

In October of 1965, he was hospitalized at the Sunrise Hospital for about four weeks and then allowed to go home. He had cancer . . . Wild Bill had to be braver now than he had ever been on the screen . . . He carried on his weekly television program (station KORK-TV in Las Vegas, Nevada) as long as he was able, but on Friday evening of November 26, 1965, at the age of 61, he passed away. (*Wrangler's Roost* article by John Hall.)

BILL ELLIOTT'S PERSONAL LIFE

Bill Elliott was a great friend of mine. After his career had ended, he came into court, having trouble in his household. He was living with a good-looking young woman. The woman had two small children, all living in the ranch house together. Bill and the woman were not married at this time. In those days, you didn't do such a thing. I was bailiff of the Superior Court at this time. Bill came into my court, and spotted me in a sheriff's uniform. He exclaimed "Bob, what are you doing in that uniform?" He grabbed me and hugged me, having not seen me in years. He said, "I have a little trouble Bob, and I'm worried sick. I said, "Bill, I will take care of you, old buddy." I talked to the judge, and he cleaned up Bill's household. Bill grabbed me again, and started to cry on my shoulder." (Bob Brown, leather crafter for many Western stars.)

Western Star Admits Love Affair With Model

Western movie star "Wild Bill" Elliott today admitted a love affair with an attractive model. It came to light during Superior Court scrutiny of a child-custody battle. The model, Mrs. Dolly Moore, 28, told Acting Superior Judge Victor J. Hayek that she and her two children had lived with Elliott at one of his ranches near Wells, Nevada. Asked if she did not realize she was violating the Seventh Commandment, which forbids adultery, she answered: "It was not as bad as abandoning my children." Mrs. Moore said she was in dire financial straits, and turned to Elliott, who is 55, for help. She said he loved her, and wanted to

Elliott and his second wife, Dolly, and her two children, Corky and Debbie, at their Las Vegas condominium.

marry her, but could not because he was married. Elliott said he has been separated for two years from Mrs. Helen Elliott, his wife of 33 years, who recently filed suit for divorce here. He has just begun a divorce action in Nevada. Asked if he believed in the Seventh Commandment, Elliott testified: "I do not." Elliott said he had read the Bible nightly to young William

Moore Jr., 9, and Deborah, 7, but in reading the Ten Commandments, omitted the seventh. Attorney Emmet Lavery asked him: "Do you think these children should be taught anything about adultery?" "I think when they are old enough," he answered, "they will think for themselves, and make up their own minds." The children's father, William Moore, 29, graduate student in mathematics at Northwestern University, took the children home with him to Evanston, Illinois, last June. At today's hearing, he was granted full custody, with the proviso that Mrs. Moore may have them seven weeks each summer if she is not "domiciled" (living) with Elliott unless they are married. (*The Knoxville Journal* circa 1959)

(Author's Note: The following details about Elliott's divorce and personal life were provided to me by a person who was a friend of Dolly Elliott and who wishes to remain anonymous. While I

Elliott and wife, Dolly, on the set of his TV show in Las Vegas.

have complete confidence in the credibility of the person supplying this information, I must point out it that it comes from Dolly's point of view.)

First of all about Bill and Helen's divorce: Helen was a very strong-willed woman who tried to run Bill's life. She was very jealous of him, not only about women but the time Bill spent with his rodeo buddies.

Dolly Moore and her first husband had a house on top of a hill which overlooked some of Bill's land he was trying to sell. Bill went to Dolly's house, and asked her if he could bring clients up to her land so they could look down on the property he had for sale. She agreed and that's how they met. Within a few weeks Bill sold his land, and offered to take Dolly and her husband out to dinner to thank them. At the time, Dolly and her husband were having trouble, mostly about her leaving the children for her modeling work. Dolly's husband also suspicioned Bill had been making a play for Dolly because he had come to their house so much. Anyway, Dolly's husband left her, and she had no money, so Bill came to her rescue and helped her with expenses. When Helen found out, the stuff hit the fan, and she and Bill split. Bill then turned to Dolly. They moved to a ranch in Nevada that had once belonged to Joel McCrea. Bill's friend Chuck Ryaan was the one who talked Joel into selling the ranch to Bill. They moved there, and tried to make a life together. Both were waiting for their divorces to become final so they could be married. However, Dolly's husband and Bill's wife got together, and conspired to file suit for him to get custody of the children. He did gain custody, but after Bill and Dolly married, Dolly regained custody.

More about the ranch purchase: When Bill decided he wanted to buy the ranch from Joel McCrea, he sent Chuck Ryaan to make the deal for him. Bill made a down payment with the remainder to be paid in a few months. When it became time to pay off the note, Bill discovered that Helen had taken all of his money from the bank. When McCrea failed to get his money, he threatened to sue Bill. Dolly said this was the only time she had seen Bill get angry. He got so upset that he put his fist through a wall. When he realized what he had done, he broke down, and cried, and apologized to Dolly. Bill and Dolly then moved to Las Vegas where her parents bought them a condominium.

It has been reported that Bill was so broke he sold his guns to a stranger on the street. This is not true. Dolly said she has no idea as to how this story got started. When Bill married Dolly, he married into one of the richest families in Las Vegas. She also said that Bill's guns were on display at a friend's bar and restaurant at the time of Bill's death. The guns then disappeared, and she never learned what happened to them.

Some have also claimed that Bill was so broke he had to get a job selling used cars. This is not true either. Bill became part owner of a car lot, spokesman for the Thunderbird lounge, and had his own TV show, while Dolly continued to model. She and Bill loved to dance, and would often be out dancing until the wee hours of the morning.

When Bill and Helen divorced, their daughter Barbara sided with her mother. She had little to do with Bill from then on. Although Bill gave Barbara a car for her birthday the year before he died, Barbara did not come to see him when she was informed that he was terminally ill. She did not come to see him the day of his funeral. She flew in from New York, and went straight to the funeral home for a short while. She never spoke to Dolly or took part in the service, which Dolly said was one of the largest ever held in Las Vegas. Barbara never asked about a will. It was like she had come only because it was expected. Bill loved Barbara very much, but his love was not returned after the divorce. Bill's first wife did not send flowers or acknowledge the death because of her continued hatred for him.

After Bill's death, Dolly bought a house across the street from the Tropicana Hotel, right next door to Betty Gable's house—on the other side was Paul Anka's. She lived there for several years before the MGM Company bought all these houses. Dolly did not want to sell but was forced to when all her neighbors sold out. The MGM Hotel and Casino now stands where the houses once stood. I don't know where she moved because her family is very protective of her. She used to phone me on New Year's; perhaps she will next year.

(Author's Note: Bill Elliott was not a perfect man—no one is—but his good qualities far surpassed his bad ones. He was a hero to millions of youngsters, and he was admired and respected by everyone who worked with him. He was apparently sorry and repentant for some things he had done in his life. As proof, I offer the following quote by Bill's pastor):

At this point in the story, I bring in The Reverend Harry Finkenstaedt, an American clergyman now living in England. He knew Bill very well at the time, and he recently wrote to me the following: "I knew Bill Elliott in Las Vegas in 1960 when I was a curate at Christ Church on Maryland Avenue. He came to that Episcopal Church most Sundays, and we became friends. He was a very clean-cut looking man, always smartly suited up and made a handsome figure. I remember him as being very caring and considerate. Also, he was contrite about some things in his past life, and wanted to have a clean slate and do everything as 'right' as he could. He believed in God and Christ, and asked to be, and was, baptized by me. I thought he was a thoroughly kind, thoughtful person, and he was quite charming." So, whatever Bill's feelings of guilt were about we shall never know. But he had faced up to them and continued living in Las Vegas. (*Wrangler's Roost* article by John M. Hall.)

BILL ELLIOTT OBITUARY

(Born October 16, 1904; died November 26, 1965)

(Author's Note: some sources report Elliott being born in 1903, 1904 and 1905. His death certificates says 1904.)

Las Vegas, Nevada, November 27, 1965—Wild Bill Elliott, the Western movie and television actor, who was once voted one of the 10 leading money-makers in Westerns, died yesterday of cancer. He was 62 years old. William Elliott, who had starred in more than 60 sagebrush sagas, was nicknamed "Wild Bill" after he was cast as Wild Bill Hickok in a 1938 movie serial. It was estimated that he disposed of more badmen than all the frontier marshals together. He also appeared as Red Ryder in a series that began in 1944. Square-jawed, rangy, laconic Wild Bill was a natural recruit for his roles on the range. He could ride a horse, was fast on the draw, and seemed equally adept at throwing lead or punches. He departed from what had become the standard type of movie cowboy, however, by never carrying a guitar or bursting into a song. He also frequently kissed his leading lady with ardor. "I guess," he once remarked, "I helped invent the adult Western. But, luckily, the kids never noticed." A perfectionist, he practiced riding tricks, fancy shooting, and roping. Mr. Elliott was born on a ranch in Pattonsburg, Missouri, learned riding and roping at the stock yards in Kansas City, where his father worked, and later entered rodeos there. He studied acting at the Pasadena (California) Playhouse, and early in his career appeared in non-western dramatic film. His picture credits included IN OLD SACRAMENTO, PLAINSMAN AND THE LADY, WYOMING, THE FABULOUS TEXAN, and OLD LOS ANGELES. He is survived by his widow, the former Dolly Moore, who was a model, and a daughter, Barbara, by his first marriage to Mrs. Helen Elliott, which ended in divorce.

A late publicity photo of Elliott.

BILL ELLIOTT'S PRINCIPAL SIDEKICKS

DUB "CANNONBALL" TAYLOR

One doesn't have to see Dub "Cannonball" Taylor to recognize him. His great Southern accent, and his high-pitched giggle make him instantly recognizable. It is surprising how little is written about Taylor, since he appeared as a sidekick in nearly 50 cowboy films. He was in films with two of the all-time great Western stars, "Wild Bill" Elliott and Charles "Durango" Starrett. He also worked with Don "Red" Barry, Russell Hayden, and Jimmy Wakely. Yet when one peruses the reference books, magazines, and articles written about that fascinating era, there is hardly more than a casual mention of Taylor. Many Western fans wonder how Taylor could have been so overlooked. Perhaps the answer lies with Taylor himself. He let it be known for years that he was not proud of his B-Western participation, and did not want to be called "Cannonball." Regardless of his assessment of his work and Western historians' opinions, history should not be ignored because Dub Taylor is one of the beloved characters who made us laugh during our youthful years at the Saturday matinees.

Walter "Dub" Taylor was born in Richmond, Virginia, on Feburary 26, 1909. As a youngster, he lived in Augusta, Georgia, and Greenville, South Carolina. He finally wound up in

Oklahoma City where he spent his teenage years. He attended Classen High School in Oklahoma City where he often entertained the students with the harmonica and the xylophone. When he was in his late teens, he was discovered by Larry Rich, a vaudeville star, and invited to go to New York. The New Yorkers liked his act, and although they could not understand much of what he said, they enjoyed the way he said it. They had never heard words pronounced in such a manner and with so thick an accent. If Taylor enjoyed his stay in New York as much as they did, he must have had a good time. One of the great events in Taylor's life happened on that trip. He met his wife Florence Dean, who was also in show business. Unlike many show-business marriages, this one lasted for over 50 years. They had two children, Faydean and Buck. Many Western fans remember Buck as the character "Newley O'Brien" on the long running television series "Gunsmoke".

Although better known as a Western sidekick, Dub Taylor made

Buck Taylor, author Bobby Copeland, and Dub "Cannonball" Taylor at the 1986 Knoxville Film Festival.

an auspicious film debut by appearing in the 1938 Columbia classic YOU CAN'T TAKE IT WITH YOU. The film featured Jimmy Stewart and Jean Arthur. The movie won an Oscar for the best picture and director for that year. The renowned Frank Capra directed Taylor in the film, and was very impressed by Taylor's acting skills. In his autobiography, *The Name Above The Title*, he had this to say about Dub Taylor: "That left just one more daffy part to cast—Ed, Essie's xylophone-playing husband. I was interviewing xylophone players when in walked a merry oaf wearing a perpetual infectious grin as big as a sunburst. Sweat drops gleamed on his receding forehead. 'I'm Dub Taylor, suh, and I kin play the xylophone.' His very presence evoked laughter. "Have you ever played in a picture, Mr. Taylor?" I asked. 'No suh, I ain't. But I played in the Rose Bowl on the Alabama football team' (jokingly). His Southern accent dripped like hominy grits. I asked him to play the xylophone that I had in the office.

'I'll play you a love song, Mr. Capra. I'll play you "Dinah."' "The uproar he raised on the xylophone would wake the dead. He made "Dinah" sound like four anvil choruses. The louder I laughed, the louder he played. I cast him on the spot."

Capra also used Taylor in the Bing Crosby film RIDING HIGH. Capra, in writing about Crosby and Taylor and the rest of the cast, said that he had "put together one of the greatest collections of time-saving, sure-fire entertainers ever assembled in one film." Taylor is proud of his association with Capra and many times has said, "Frank Capra is one fine gentleman and the best director that I ever worked for."

After Taylor's success with Frank Capra, Columbia decided that Taylor would make a good Western sidekick, and cast him with their relatively new cowboy hero, Bill Elliott. Taylor's first film in the series was THE TAMING OF THE WEST, issued in 1939. He continued with Elliott through the 1941 film KING OF

DODGE CITY. This film also featured Tex Ritter. During the filming of the Elliott series, Taylor did take time out to do a film for Republic called ONE MAN'S LAW starring Don "Red" Barry. He was replaced in the Elliott films by comic Frank Mitchell. Mitchell also assumed the name Cannonball. Many fans feel the name was inappropriate for Mitchell, and that the studio should have created a new name more in tune with the Mitchell character. Perhaps "Dropsey" would have been a better name for Mitchell since most of his comedy consisted of him stumbling or falling using the acrobatic skills he had learned earlier in his career.

Following his work with Elliott, Columbia teamed Taylor with Russell Hayden, formerly of the "Hopalong Cassidy" films. He appeared as Cannonball in eight films with Hayden. SILVER CITY RAIDERS was one of the better entries in the Hayden series, and Taylor was at his best in that film.

After his stint with Hayden, he joined the popular Charles Starrett series in 1943. It is notable that while working with Starrett, The Durango Kid character was revived. The first Durango Kid film was made in 1940, but for some mysterious reason, Columbia did not see fit to continue with the series at that time. Undoubtedly, that was a mistake, for the series has proven to be one of the most popular B-Western series ever filmed. Taylor worked with Starrett until the 1946 film FRONTIER LAW. At that time, Smiley Burnette, who had been a very popular sidekick to Gene Autry, was brought in to replace Taylor. Starrett had been pleased with Taylor's work, and has told of his displeasure over Taylor's departure.

In 1947, Monogram decided Lee "Lasses" White was getting too old to continue his sidekick role in the Jimmy Wakely films. Monogram learned of Taylor's availability, and quickly signed him for the role. Taylor, again as Cannonball, appeared in 15 Wakely films. He did not do his best work in the Wakely series.

Wakely was a rather low-key individual, and White had provided him with comedy that matched Wakely's style. Taylor's slapstick style did not suit Wakely and set well with many of Wakely's fans. Taylor stayed through the last film in the series, which was LAWLESS CODE, filmed in 1949.

Many actors who performed in the B-Westerns found acting jobs difficult to find when that era came to an end. Taylor, however, became more prosperous, appearing in many "A" productions. His later films included (films are listed in no particular order) CRIME WAVE, THE UNDEFEATED, THE BOUNTY HUNTER, NO TIME FOR SERGEANTS, THE WILD BUNCH, THE HALLELUJAH TRAIL, DEATH OF A GUNSLINGER, A HOLE IN THE HEAD, PARRISH, SWEET BIRD OF YOUTH, BONNIE AND CLYDE, BANDOLERO!, A MAN CALLED HORSE, THE REIVERS, SUPPORT YOUR LOCAL GUNFIGHTER!, and THE WILD COUNTRY. In those films, he appeared with such movie greats as Dean Martin, Warren Beatty, Burt Lancaster, Richard Harris, Randolph Scott, James Stewart, James Garner, and John Wayne. He had an important role in BONNIE AND CLYDE. The film really gave Taylor a chance to show the audiences he was truly a fine actor.

In 1957, Taylor was a regular on the TV series "Casey Jones", which starred Alan Hale, Jr., of "Gilligan's Island" fame. The series also featured another former B-Western sidekick, Eddy Waller. Waller was noted for the role of Nugget Clark in the Allan "Rocky" Lane series. Taylor was hired for another TV series in the mid-sixties called "Please Don't Eat The Daisies".

It seemed that through the years he continued to pop up in various roles in just about every television series. Taylor was obviously well-liked and a highly respected actor, or he, like many of his B-Western counterparts, would have faded into oblivion.

At a 1984 film festival, Charles "Durango" Starrett told an audience about Taylor "Oh, Dub Taylor! I just loved Dub. I wish he could have continued in my films. Dub was a great sidekick and a fine actor. He still is. We used to go hunting together; he's a fine shot. I see him all the time on television. I'm very proud of his accomplishments. He's one of the finest character actors around; and, like I said, I wish he could have continued in my films."

In Charlotte, North Carolina, at a 1986 festival, I talked with writer-producer-director Oliver Drake. I asked Drake about Dub Taylor. Drake exclaimed, "Well, I only worked with Dub Taylor on the Jimmy Wakely films at Monogram. Perhaps someone else could tell you more about him than I can. I will tell you that I had no problems with him. I honestly feel that Dub thought he was destined for greater things than that of a Western sidekick. He got such a terrific start, you know, in the great Capra film. He doesn't want to be called Cannonball, and I think that he would like people to forget his role in the B-Westerns. (Drake's remarks were made after the 1986 festival, held in Knoxville, Tennessee, where Taylor freely referred to himself as Cannonball.)

It was a great victory for Western fans when, in April 1986, the Knoxville Western Film Caravan persuaded Taylor to be a guest at the festival. Taylor, for years, had let it be known that he had no interest in the festivals. He wanted people to forget his Cannonball characterization, and refused to be called by that name. After much coaxing to attend, he mentioned that his grandchildren had never seen his Western work. He was immediately sent some video tapes, and the grandchildren loved them. The next contact with Taylor found him more receptive. (It seems the best way to reach a grandfather's heart is still through the eyes of his grandchildren.) Still, he would not give an affirmative reply. He did say, "If I decide to come, I will let you know; and when I tell someone I will do something, I will do it." After some more calls, he consented to come if he could bring his son, Buck. The festival officials were delighted, and considered Buck a real addition to the event.

Even though Taylor agreed to attend the festival, and his appearance was announced in all the trade publications, many Western fans were still doubtful if he would show. Show he did and what a guest! Buck warned that his father had only one speed and that was wide-open. He told officials, "If you want him for the entire festival, you will have to pace him for he will wear himself out on the first day." Buck was taken at his word, and Dub was cared for so that he could participate in some of the activities each day.

Dub's entrance for the first panel discussion saw him bellow out with that ever familiar voice, "Howdy folks, Cannonball he'ah!" The fans loved it, and he was given a tremendous ovation. Taylor was wildly entertaining, making one funny remark after another. He had the audience roaring with his wisecracks and jokes. He reminisced about his pictures with Starrett, Elliott, and Hayden. He said nothing about the Wakely films. Perhaps it was because those films were produced by Monogram, and they did not have the production value of the films produced by Columbia. It could have been because Jimmy Wakely made it known that, although he liked Taylor, he did not like Taylor's type of comedy for his films.

Taylor continued to participate in various phases of the festival by posing for pictures and signing hundreds of autographs. He seemed like he was genuinely having a good time. He was asked about the origination of the name Cannonball. He replied, "I really don't know, the studio gave it to me. Maybe it's because I'm short and kinda round," patting himself on the stomach.

The fans were touched by the affection Buck and Dub demonstrated for one another. Dub bragged on Buck at every opportunity, and Buck said of Dub, "He looked after me when I was growing up, and I'm going to take care of him now."

Dub Taylor told the fans that he enjoyed working and said, "I'll never retire. I've got too many expensive hobbies. As long as I can make people happy and laugh and get in some hunting and fishing, I just might live to be a hundred." True to his word, Taylor remained active until he passed away on October 3, 1994, of congestive heart failure. He was 87 years old.

FRANK MITCHELL—THE OTHER CANNONBALL

Frank Mitchell, who appeared as the comic sidekick in the Bill Elliott-Tex Ritter series made for Columbia Pictures in 1941-42, passed away on January 21, 1991. He died at the Laurelwood Convalescent Hospital in North Hollywood of cardiac arrest. Mitchell replaced Dub Taylor as the "Cannonball" character, and appeared in seven of the Elliott-Ritter movies: BULLETS FOR BANDITS, THE DEVIL'S TRAIL, THE LONE STAR VIGILANTES, NORTH OF THE ROCKIES, PRAIRIE GUNSMOKE, ROARING FRONTIERS, and VENGEANCE OF THE WEST.

The diminutive Mitchell must not have made much of an impact on the fans as a cowboy comic because he did not appear in any more B-Western movies after the conclusion of the Elliott-Ritter series.

A few years ago, Frank Mitchell was one of the guest celebrities at the Knoxville Western Film Festival. It was there that I obtained the following information:

Q. You weren't a real cowboy, were you?

A. Oh no, I was a dude from New York. I was pretty green about cowboys and making Westerns until I got the job doing them. I had a lot of fun working in Westerns.

Q. I understand that you had been in show business a long time before you made the cowboy films?

A. You bet, I was in a touring vaudeville act when I was 12

Frank Mitchell, the other "Cannonball."

years old. I was an acrobat, and did Charlie Chaplin imitations even before that. It was because of my acrobatic skills that I was asked to join the vaudeville tour. I could fall all over the place without hurting myself. Taking falls is not as easy as it looks. If you don't know what you are doing, you can break your neck.

Q. When were you born?

A. May 13, 1905, in New York City.

Q. Tell me more about your vaudeville career.

A. I worked in vaudeville a number of years and with several different groups and partners. While working out at the gym one day, I met a fellow named Jack Durant. He was also an acrobat. We became friends, and decided to develop an act and team up. It was a routine that you wouldn't believe. It was really pretty rough, especially for me. We would slap, kick, push, trip, punch, and fall all over the stage. Since I was the little guy, we thought that it would be more effective if I was on the receiving end of the action. I don't mind telling you that some mornings it was a little difficult getting out of bed. I never really got hurt, but you couldn't help getting some bruises once in a while. I always kept in good shape for the routine, and that helped me perform without getting injured. The Mitchell and Durant team because quite successful and famous. We played Broadway and even at the Palladium in London, England. In 1934, we signed a movie contract with Fox Studios, and made some musicals with Alice Faye. Durant and I broke up a short time later, and I decided to go it alone. I then signed up to do THE SINGING KID with Al Jolsen. During the years that followed, I must have worked for all the major studios and with some of Hollywood's biggest stars.

Q. With such a background, how did you get into making films with Bill Elliott and Tex Ritter?

A. I had worked in a couple of Westerns before I started working in movies with Bill and Tex. In 1940, I did a film with Tex called RHYTHM OF THE RIO GRANDE. That same year, I worked with Johnny Mack Brown and Bob Baker in WEST OF CARSON CITY. So I did have a little experience in Westerns. Well, in 1941, an agent named Mitch Hamilburg called me, and said that Dub Taylor was leaving the Elliott-Ritter series. He knew that I was about Dub's size, and could do the same things that he had been doing. Mitch talked to Columbia, and I was given the part. I didn't even have to try out for it because the studio was familiar with my work.

Q. Tell me about Bill Elliott and Tex Ritter.

A. They were both great guys and easy to work with; everyone liked them. You couldn't ask to be around two finer people. They not only got along with everyone, but they were hard workers.

Q. Was there any jealously between Elliott and Ritter?

A. None that I could see. I'm sure that they would have liked to have been starring in their own series instead of sharing the billing, but who wouldn't? I never saw any jealousy or heard any unkind words. They were quality gentlemen with a job to do, and they did it well. I'm sure that anyone who ever worked with Bill and Tex would tell you the same thing.

Q. How about Johnny Mack Brown and Bob Baker?

A. I liked Johnny; he was a real gentleman. He had that great Southern accent and was such a fine looking fellow. I don't remember anything about Baker.

Q. How did you get along with the other cowboy sidekicks?

A. I didn't know any except Dub Taylor. We were both with Columbia for a while.

Q. Can you think of some amusing or unusual thing that happened to you while making Westerns?

A. There's probably a lot of amusing things that I could tell you. One thing does stand out in my mind: it seems that the fellows were always looking for a prank to pull on the new guy on the set. Well, they brought me this beautiful white stallion to ride. I thought it was a little strange that they would give a guy like me such a beautiful horse. I climbed aboard, and took off on him right in front of the whole crew. About that time, someone started playing a record of the "Star Spangled Banner". When the horse heard that music, it reared up and started pawing the air, and doing all kinds of shenanigans. I had to hang on for dear life. The horse had been a circus performer, and had been trained to act up when that song was played. I'll never forget that experience!

Q. What did you do after the conclusion of the Elliott-Ritter films?

A. I continued making movies for several years. I worked with such people as Esther Williams, Red Skelton, Stewart Granger, Glenn Ford, and Martin and Lewis. I also worked in television on shows like "Boston Blackie" and "Wagon Train". I had a long career in show business, and enjoyed every minute of it. After leaving the business, I started selling real estate.

Q. Are you enjoying the festival?

A. You bet, this is a great place and everyone has been swell to me.

(Author' Note: I'm sure Frank Mitchell must have been excellent as a vaudeville performer, and perhaps quite good in some of his movie roles. However, I do not rate him outstanding as a cowboy sidekick. In fact, I don't even think he was mediocre. I do consider the Elliott-Ritter series to be among the finest B-Western films ever made, but I thought the movies would have been even better without Mitchell's presence. I found him totally unfunny, and his work was so repetitious that after seeing him in a couple of films, one could easily predict his next pratfall. His attempt at being funny reminded me a lot of Pinky Lee who tried to provide comedy for Roy Rogers in his final three films. Both Mitchell and Lee were short in stature and, in my opinion, woefully weak as cowboy comics.

I am glad I got the opportunity to meet Frank Mitchell, for I found him to be a very pleasant man, and far more amusing in person than he was in his Western films. He seemed to genuinely enjoy meeting the film festival fans.

Despite my opinion of Mitchell's performance as a cowboy sidekick, he was a participant in the exciting and nostalgic era of B-Western films. And that alone should endear him to the hearts of the enthusiasts who still have an appreciation for these grand old movies.)

GABBY HAYES
contributed by John A. Rutherford

"You dirty . . . !" growls the grubby old, bewhiskered character named Coyote as he is shot fatally in the stomach by the villain, Morgan Conway. Unthinkable! How can lovable, old Gabby Hayes be killed off in the Randolph Scott Western, BADMAN'S TERRITORY (1946, RKO)? It was not often that Gabby was dispatched in such a manner. He was a durable character who could trace his roots back to the early Westerns. In fact, he appeared as an extra in many films prior to his first real part in the film, BIG NEWS (1929, Pathe). Before that, he had spent 28 years on the stage in vaudeville. In the twenties, he came to Hollywood.

George Francis Hayes was born on May 7, 1885 in Wellsville, New York. In 1914, he married Olive Ireland. Later, after is first wife died, he married Dorothy Earle, an actress.

To many Western film fans, Gabby was the favorite comic side-kick of all time. In the Motion Picture Herald-Fame Poll, he was voted one of the ten best Money-Making Western Stars from 1943-1952 and 1954. After all, he worked with the likes of Bob Steele, John Wayne, Ken Maynard, William Boyd, Gene Autry, Roy Rogers, Wild Bill Elliott, and Randolph Scott, to name a few.

From 1929 to 1933, he appeared in a variety of pictures, including Westerns. In 1931, he was in NEVADA BUCKAROO (Tiffany) with Bob Steele. Other Bob Steele films followed until 1933. That year he was cast with Randolph Scott in the Zane Grey Western, WILD HORSE MESA (Paramount).

Also, in 1933, Hayes began a series of Westerns with John Wayne in which he often played a villain, most notably in RANDY RIDES ALONE (1934, Monogram). He was dressed all in black and clean shaven as he got the drop on John Wayne. In one of these films, THE LUCKY TEXAN (1934, Monogram), Hayes foreshadowed his comic talents in a sidekick role, preparing for his future character roles.

He took a part in a singing cowboy Ken Maynard film, for Mascot in 1934, which was significant only because it introduced Gene Autry and Smiley Burnette, entitled IN OLD SANTA FE.

His first big break came in 1935, a banner year in B-Westerns,

Elliott with Gabby Hayes and badman Harry Woods (BORDERTOWN GUN FIGHTERS, Republic, 1944).

in which he was cast as Uncle Ben, a lovable codger, in the film HOP-A-LONG CASSIDY (Paramount) who was killed by the villain towards the end. Reviewers were unfavorable toward the needless killing off of a popular character. In his second Hopalong film, Hayes was cast as a bartender, a less sympathetic role, but again he was killed off.

It was in the third Hoppy film, BAR 20 RIDES AGAIN (1935, Paramount), that Hayes introduced his "Windy Halliday" character into the series, playing a desert rat who befriends Hopalong. He is allowed to live through the film and, at the end, joins the Bar-20 hands as a regular character. Because his character became so popular quickly, the film series skipped his "Windy" character for one film, but from then on "Windy" became the permanent comic sidekick to William Boyd and James Ellison.

However, in 1935, Hayes appeared in two other Westerns, Zane Grey's THUNDER MOUNTAIN (Fox) with George O'Brien, and TUMBLING TUMBLEWEEDS (Repubic) with Gene Autry. Hayes also took a respite in the Frank Capra comedy, MR. DEEDS GOES TO TOWN (1936, Columbia), with Gary Cooper. He also had a character role in a John Wayne film, THE LAWLESS NINETIES (1936, Republic). Hayes played Major Carter, the father of the heroine—a migratory editor from Virginia who is mildly pompous. He is shot down during a fight staged to get him for writing editorials against the villain.

As "Breezy", he was cast in the DeMille epic Western in 1937, THE PLAINSMAN.) Meanwhile, he continued as "Windy" in the Hopalong films. He made several non-westerns in 1937 and 1938. He played "Grandpappy" in the Bob Burns film, MOUNTAIN MUSIC (1937, Paramount). He was also cast as the Man with the Bowler Hat in EMIL, a British film based upon a children's story, *Emil and the Detective* in 1938. In this most unusual role, Hayes drugs a boy on a train and steals his money. He also played Captain Strozzi in the Jimmy Durante musical, FORBIDDEN MUSIC (1938, World Wide).

In 1938, Hayes made his last film in the Hopalong series, SILVER ON THE SAGE (Paramount), leaving to go to Republic Studios as a regular. It has been suggested that he left the series because he felt William Boyd was too difficult to work with. "Bill Boyd was a tough guy to work with. Finally, George Hayes said he couldn't stand it anymore, so he went to work at Republic with Roy Rogers." (This remark is attributed to Russell Hayden in *They Went That Away* by James Horwitz.). That his absence was felt was obvious since the "Windy" role was retired like a famous baseball player's uniform, and a new character was developed for the series—that of "California" Carlson as portrayed by Andy Clyde.

At Republic, Hayes was cast in FIGHTING THROUGHBREDS

(1939), and then loaned to MGM for the part of "Pop" Wilkie in LET FREEDOM RING (1939) with Nelson Eddy. Back at Republic, he was assigned to their big Western epic of 1939, MAN OF CONQUEST, with Richard Dix—the story of Sam Houston. He also appeared in the Gene Autry film, IN OLD MONTEREY (Republic) with Smiley Burnette.

A second big break came for Hayes when he was scheduled to replace Raymond Hatton in the new Roy Rogers series in the film, IN OLD CALIENTE (1939, Republic). As Rogers developed, so did Hayes in his new character, "Gabby", the cantankerous, old, bewhiskered, but lovable comic sidekick. Several other Rogers' films followed, developing the "Gabby" character.

DARK COMMAND, Republic's 1940 epic Western, provided Hayes with a role as "Doc Grunch," a relief from "Gabby". In 1940, he also appeared in an unusual Western, WAGONS WESTWARD (Republic) starring Chester Morris and Buck Jones. He played a grizzled old swamper named "Hardtack."

In 1940, he was in the Autry film, MELODY RANCH (Republic), with Jimmy Durante and Vera Vague. Meanwhile, his Rogers' films continued with "Gabby" faithfully backing Roy. Hayes made two non-westerns in 1941. He played a policeman in the Columbia film, THE VOICE IN THE NIGHT, and appeared with Helen Hayes in an English film, FRIGHTENED LADY.

Smiley Burnette was teamed with Hayes in the 1942 Rogers film, HEART OF THE GOLDEN WEST (Republic). Following the Rogers film, RIDIN' DOWN THE CANYON (1942, Republic), Hayes left the series for a while.

"Wild Bill" Elliott had come over to Republic from Columbia, and Gabby was scheduled as a co-star with Anne Jeffreys in the Elliott series, beginning with the film, CALLING WILD BILL ELLIOTT (1943). Seven more in this series followed the same year. In 1944, Elliott was cast in the "Red Ryder" series, and Hayes continued with him, co-starring with Alice Fleming as the "Duchess" and Bobby Blake as "Little Beaver." Hayes was a non-comic strip character who was constantly bickering with the Duchess. However, after two films in this series, TUCSON RAIDERS and MARSHAL OF RENO, Hayes departed. Also in 1943, Hayes had been cast in a John Wayne film, IN OLD OKLAHOMA (Republic).

In 1944, he received a part as Dave in the big John Wayne's Western, TALL IN THE SADDLE (RKO). Following this, he returned to the Rogers series in LIGHTS OF OLD SANTA FE (1944, Republic). He was also cast in the film, THE BIG BONANZA (1944, Republic), with Richard Arlen and Robert Livingston.

Perhaps his biggest role came in the 1945 Roy Rogers film, DON'T FENCE ME IN (Republic). The Cole Porter title song was a huge success, and helped the film also to be a big hit. Gabby played a retired outlaw, presumed dead who is discovered and accused of murder. Following this film, Gabby was at the height of his popularity. His last film with Rogers was HELDORADO (1946, Republic).

In his next film, Hayes appeared with Randolph Scott as "Coyote" in BADMAN'S TERRITORY (1946, RKO). He followed this with a role in TRAIL STREET (1947, RKO), another Randolph Scott film. Reviewers were not so kind to this film, including Gabby's role.

He also made a non-western film, GREAT EXPECTATIONS (1947, Universal), playing Compeyson, another out-of-character role for him, which he did often in his career.

Returning to Westerns he was cast as "Windy" Gibson in the big Republic Western, WYOMING (1947) with Bill Elliott. Then he was reunited with Russell Hayden in the Randolph Scott Western ALBUQUERQUE (1948, Paramount). In 1948, he also made RETURN OF THE BAD MEN (RKO), another Scott film, and THE UNTAMED BREED at Columbia. He was cast as "Pesky" in EL PASO (1949, Paramount), starring three Western actors, John Payne, Sterling Hayden, and Dick Foran. His last film was CARIBOU TRAIL (1950, 20th-Fox), a Scott film in which he played a sourdough who has a pesky donkey. The final fadeout had him and his donkey on the mountain in the setting sun. A perfect finish to a long and respectable career as the best comic sidekick in Western film history. Perhaps, it was said best by Don Miller in *Hollywood Corral*: "Hayes refined the art of playing the foil, gave it humility, and a cantankerous dignity."

(Author's Note: Hayes passed away on February 9, 1969.)

BOBBY "LITTLE BEAVER" BLAKE

Bobby Blake portrayed an orphaned, Navajo Indian child who became a ward of Red Ryder in a total of 23 entries in the very popular series—16 with Bill Elliott and seven with Allan Lane. He had a much more significant part in the Elliott features than he did in those with Lane. Perhaps this was because Elliott was known to have liked children, and apparently Lane liked no one but Lane. Through the years, Blake has commented on his wonderful relationship and his admiration of Elliott, while, at the same time, candidly, expressing his dislike for Lane.

Peggy Stewart, who played in the "Red Ryder" pictures with Elliott, Lane, and Jim Bannon, and who was once married to another Red Ryder, Don Barry, said of Blake, "Bobby was such a practical joker. He would put gravel in your boots, and do other pranks. It was never dull with Bobby around. He hated to wear that feather, oh, how he hated that darned feather. He would hide from the hair dresser until the last minute. A few years ago, I visited Bobby on the set of his TV show. I slipped onto the set a Red Ryder lobby card where he could easily spot it. Shortly afterwards, I heard him give a big war whoop, and he came running to find me. We had a wonderful reunion. He got me a part in both of his TV series, 'Helltown' and 'Baretta'. I guess I should call him Robert now."

Bobby Blake was born Michael Gubitosi on September 18, 1933, in Nutley, New Jersey. He started out as a child actor in the very popular "Our Gang" comedy shorts in the late 1930s and 1940s. He worked in the series for some five years, playing, a character called Mickey, which was his nickname in real life. Unlike some of the children in the "Our Gang" series who were comical to look at, or had other peculiarities, Blake was a beautiful child and pretty much played a normal youngster in the films.

Blake started the "Red Ryder" series in 1944, when he was only 10 years old. He was more than an adequate rider for his age, and, in all 23 of the Ryder entries he rode a horse called Papoose.

It was while as Little Beaver that he also made two color B-Westerns at Republic with Monte Hale. Six months later, after departing Republic, Bobby was cast as another Indian boy for the big-budget THE ROUND-UP (1947), Gene Autry's initial film for Columbia. He also appeared in A-Westerns and other large production features most notably as the kid who sold Humphrey Bogart the winning lottery ticket in THE TREASURE OF THE SIERRA MADRE.

Through the years, Blake racked up a list of professional credits. He also developed a reputation as a difficult actor, one prone to drinking and drugs and wild behavior. Such behavior cost Blake numerous roles because no one wanted to work with him. Blake blames a lot of his antics on his treatment by his parents. He claimed he had been abused physically and sexually as a child. He said of his father, "My father hated my success. He wanted to be there instead of me, and if not him,

Bobby Blake appeared in 23 Red Ryder pictures.

This photo was taken while Blake was appearing on stage at a theatre in Greensboro, North Carolina, during the 1940s.

then the apple of his eye—my brother. But it was me." He said of his mother, "She would invent some story about how I had misbehaved, and my father would throw me in the bedroom and beat me."

After many years in psychotherapy, he now claims to have his life in order. He ended a seven-year exile by appearing in the critically acclaimed television movie, "Judgment Day: The John List Story". Blake commented on the quality of his new life, "I love to work out, dance, sing, and play the guitar. I go to toy shows looking for the things I never had time to enjoy as a child. Life is absolutely exquisite. I wake up in the mornings, and there ain't enough hours, enough minutes, enough seconds, enough people out there for me to hug and to hug me back. And you people out there who have little, sad, frightened, scared, lost, desperate kids inside you that are fighting to live and wanting to die—you can go back there and save them just like I was lucky enough to save Mickey (himself). None of us has to be in that dark place anymore."

FRED HARMAN—COWBOY ARTIST, CREATOR OF RED RYDER

by Jim Ryan

"From out of the West comes America's famous fighting cowboy . . . Red Ryder." Thus opened the Red Ryder radio program of the 1940's. Fred Harman, the cartoonist from whose pen Red Ryder originated, was a true Westerner who successfully combined life as a rancher and as an artist. Through his Red Ryder newspaper comic strip, he brought events grounded in his authentic cowboy experience, characters based on his actual acquaintances, and the scenic natural setting of his southwest Colorado homeland to readers across the country. Expanding to other media, including storybooks, comic magazines, radio, and motion pictures, Fred Harman's characters, Red Ryder and Little Beaver, captured the hearts of millions of fans across the United States and abroad. Today, visitors to the Fred Harman Art Museum in Pagosa Springs, Colorado, can trace Fred's remarkable career and re-live memories of Red Ryder and Little Beaver.

Born in St. Joseph, Missouri, in 1902, Fred Harman was brought, at the age of two months, to the family home in Pagosa Springs, Colorado. The homestead, on which his father and uncle had filed in the 1890's, was in Indian country, part of the Apache and Ute hunting grounds. Located east of Durango, south of Creede (once home of Bat Masterson) and west of

Wolf Creek Pass, with the Rio Grande and San Juan Rivers flowing near the San Juan Mountain Range, the region is unmistakably the kind of country that inspires Western songs and stories.

In this high country, the winters tend to be long and hard. As boys, Fred and his brothers, often snowbound, are reported to have sat around the family table on many a winter's night copying illustrations from mail-order catalogs. This drawing constituted young Fred's only training as an artist. Fred was raised on the ranch and spent most of his youth and early manhood working as a cowboy in the Pagosa Springs region.

At age 18, Fred went to Kansas City, Missouri, for winter employment as a pressman's helper for the Kansas City Star, getting his first glimpse of commercial art being performed. The following winter found Fred again in Kansas City, this time at his first professional job. At the Film Ad Company, he worked as an illustrator alongside Walt Disney and Ub Iwerks, who were destined to find fame as Hollywood animators. Following failure of a joint business venture, Disney went to Hollywood and Harman returned to ranching, which he combined with work as an advertising illustrator.

In 1926, Fred married the former Lola Andrews who was to share the hardships and successes of his remaining lifetime. A son, Fred III, was born to the Harmans in 1927. Family responsibilities increased the necessity for Fred to find secure and satisfying employment. Fred traveled often in the ensuing years in search of suitable work, then settled his family in a cabin back in Colorado.

In the early 1930's, Fred began a 5-year stay in California. Although he decided against becoming an animated cartoonist in the mold of his friend Walt Disney and his brother Hugh Harman, Fred did create a Western comic strip entitled Bronc

Peeler. To market the strip, he traveled personally to newspapers in various Western towns, often paying his expenses by engaging in poker games. For a time, the strip's title character, Bronc Peeler, had a sidekick named Coyote Pete, but Mrs. Harman persuaded Fred to appeal to the younger generation by creating a youthful Indian character called Little Beaver. Bronc Peeler just didn't catch on as hoped, and Fred was forced

Don Barry and Tommy Cook (THE ADVENTURES OF RED RYDER, Republic, 1940).

to abandon the strip.

Fred then worked at various illustrating jobs, never giving up the idea of a comic strip. He produced a Whitman Big-Little Book called COWBOY LINGO, and accepted Stephen Slesinger as his agent, a pivotal career decision. In New York, in 1938, Fred got his big break. When a major comic strip syndicate expressed interest, Fred revised his earlier work to create the Red Ryder strip. He adopted the catchy new name for his hero, retained Little Beaver as Red's companion, and changed the locale of his strip from New Mexico to southwest Colorado. The strip sold to one of the country's largest syndicates, first appearing in Sunday newspaper editions in November, 1938. Daily editions soon followed, and the public took the redheaded cowpoke to their hearts.

A national phenomenon had begun. At its peak, the Red Ryder comic strip is estimated to have been seen by 45,000,000 loyal followers in over 750 newspapers on three continents. In addition, Red Ryder and Little Beaver books and comic magazines sold by the millions. In 1942, a weekly RED RYDER radio program began. Of the 40 or so products marketed with the Red Ryder endorsement, perhaps the most well-known was the Daisy Red Ryder air rifle. During the 1940's and early 1950's, Red Ryder motion pictures appeared in over 8,000 theaters, and were well-received by eager fans. It is a tribute to the durability of Fred Harman's character that Red Ryder survived movie-maker's adaptations as well as interpretation by an assortment of actors.

Hoping to capitalize on the popularity of the comic strip, Republic Studios acquired film rights to the Red Ryder property and promptly issued a 12-chapter serial, THE ADVENTURES OF RED RYDER, in 1940, starring Don "Red" Barry as Red and Tommy Cook as Little Beaver. By his own account, Barry accepted the role with great reluctance, feeling that both the serial format and the Western genre were beneath his acting talent. However, iron-willed Republic president, Herbert J. Yates, prevailed, and Don Barry became the serial Red Ryder. Although his physical stature did not compare favorably with that of the lanky comic strip hero, Don Barry's action-laden performance won great favor with matinee fans.

In 1944, Republic brought Red Ryder back to the silver screen in TUCSON RAIDERS, the first in a series of 16 feature-length films starring William "Wild Bill" Elliott, a veteran of Western serials and features. Elliott incorporated some of his personal trademarks, including his twin, reverse-holstered, bone-handled revolvers and his "I'm a peaceable man, but. . . " introduction to slam-bang action, into his Red Ryder characterization. Yet, to many fans, Elliott remains the favorite movie Red Ryder. Bowing out of the Ryder series in 1946 with SUN VALLEY CYCLONE, Elliott moved up to bigger-budgeted films.

With several Western star hopefuls reportedly under consideration to succeed Bill Elliott as Red, another serial performer, Allan Lane, was Mr. Yates' choice. Lane's athletic physique and ability to meet the action demands secured public acceptance for his Red Ryder portrayal through seven films for Republic. With RUSTLERS OF DEVIL'S CANYON in 1947, Allan Lane moved on to his own Western series and Republic concluded their Red Ryder films.

In all 23 of the Republic features, Little Beaver was played by Bobby (Robert)

Blake, who had begun his film career in the "Little Rascals" comedies and who went on to distinguish himself in such major films as IN COLD BLOOD and TELL THEM WILLIE BOY IS HERE, as well as in leading roles in television's BARETTA and HELL TOWN. In a moving speech at the Golden Boot Awards dinner in 1984, Robert Blake acknowledged his earlier repudiation of the Little Beaver role, attributing his previous attitude to a deep-seated private denial of his years as a child actor. To the delight of fans who have enjoyed his rise from child star to seasoned adult performer, Blake took this occasion to recant his earlier disdain for the role of Little Beaver. He announced his acceptance of the characterization as well as pride in his association with Western films in general. He stated that he now realized how lucky he had been for the opportunity. While other boys his age could only sit in theaters and enjoy vicariously the adventures of Red Ryder and other Western stars, he had been fortunate enough to have been there.

In his book, THE THRILL OF IT ALL, Alan G. Barbour devotes a chapter entitled "Twenty-Three Hours of Thrills" to a discussion of Republic's Red Ryder features. He rates the films as the most enjoyable B-Westerns of their time. Certainly, the Ryder films represent the staff of Republic Studios at the peak of their craft as masters of the Western action film, and the films remain popular today among collectors.

In 1949, Eagle-Lion obtained the screen rights to Red Ryder and went on to produce a series of four films starring Jim Bannon as Red and Don "Brown Jug" Reynolds as Little Beaver. In his biography, THE SON THAT ROSE IN THE WEST, Bannon credits his winning the Red Ryder role, first, to a self-promotion campaign that included driving a convertible sporting Western decor, such as steer horns and a pistol gear shift, and, secondly, to having his hair dyed red. Bannon had the further advantages of a resemblance to the comic strip hero in height, and a costume patterned closely after Fred Harman's drawings. The series was filmed in Cinecolor, and Jim Bannon made personal appearances to promote the films, but they could not match the popularity of Republic's earlier efforts. The Bannon films marked the end of Red Ryder in motion pictures. Except to collectors, the Red Ryder of the screen became just a memory.

Elliott in the first, but soon to be discarded, Red Ryder costume.

For over two decades, Fred Harman's life largely revolved around the enormous popular success of his creation, Red Ryder. Red Ryder's success dominated Fred Harman's life beyond the necessity to continuously meet comic strip deadlines. Fred acquired a ranch on 1,200 acres in Blanco Basin, on the slopes of Square Top Mountain, outside of Pagosa Springs, and built an adjacent studio from which he could look out on the Western countryside he loved. He operated the Red Ryder cattle ranch for profit, however a map of the ranch printed on the Red Ryder comic book insured there would be no privacy. Red Ryder star Jim Bannon was among the many Western celebrities who visited the ranch. At the peak of Red Ryder's popularity, up to 100 tourists and fans converged on the Red Ryder Ranch each day, causing Mrs. Harman to remark that she ran the area's largest free hotel.

Hollywood actors weren't the only ones to assume the roles of Red Ryder and Little Beaver. Fred Harman, himself, donned the Red Ryder garb and rode a black horse named Thunder. Choosing various young Indian lads from his home area to serve as Little Beaver, Fred made many personal appearances at rodeo arenas, fairs, and parades. Fans were treated to pictures of himself as Red Ryder. Without question, there was a lot of Fred Harman in Red Ryder and vice versa.

Fred's public appearances, however, weren't all as the Red Ryder character. Working with other cartoonists, Harman spent a great deal of time during World War II raising funds in bond drives, entertaining troops in both the European and Pacific theaters and visiting troop hospitals. He repeated this service during the Korean conflict.

Never content to simply create an entertaining fictional comic strip, Fred Harman had always sought to faithfully portray aspects of the real west whenever possible. Authentic scenic backgrounds of his Colorado home area served as the realistic setting for Red Ryder's comic strip adventures. To accompany his primary strip, Fred drew features such as "On the Range," "Corral of Western Lingo," and "Cowboys," which taught the language and lore of the real west.

Through his unique "News from Red Ryder Ranch" feature on the inside cover pages of the Red Ryder comic magazine, Fred shared with fans throughout the country, his real life on a Colorado ranch. A typical entry included a short, Western-flavored letter from Fred which began "Howdy Friends" or "Howdy Folks" and closed with "Adios" or "Hasta La Vista." The letterhead read, "Red Ryder Ranch, Pagosa Springs, Colorado," and depicted the cartoon Red Ryder astride Thunder reading a letter alongside the ranch mailbox marked "Blanco Basin." A half-dozen actual photographs each month, contributed from the mid to late nineteen forties by Fred's son, displayed the scenic grandeur and wildlife of the region.

Fans could enjoy sights of Indians, real cowboys herding cattle and performing ranch chores, and rodeo action, as well as the outdoor life of Fred, his family, and visitors to the ranch. The close association of real Western ranch life with the fictional Red Ryder made a lasting impression on many distant fans, including this writer as a young Eastern tenderfoot. It's little wonder that Fred Harman was credited by three Colorado governors with bringing more people to Colorado than any other individual.

While Red Ryder and Little Beaver were at the peak of their fame, Fred Harman dreamed of "riding new trails." After more than 20 years under constant pressure to meet comic strip deadlines, Fred in 1962, at the age of 60, made the difficult decision to discontinue drawing the Red Ryder comic strip. Having pursued serious Western art as a hobby periodically throughout his adult life, Fred now undertook to apply his talent to the full-time occupation of Western artist. As Harman himself explained, "I swapped saddles for the permanent satisfaction of trying always to do something better." The switch gained Fred a quieter pace, enabling him to cut back his work schedule to seven 10-hour days per week.

Artistically recreating the Western life he had experienced firsthand, Fred produced pencil sketches, watercolors, and bronze sculpture, but primarily oil paintings. His paintings received critical acclaim and became prized possessions of their purchasers. His vigorous Western scenes sparkled with action and authenticity. The realism was enhanced by his ability to recall the most minute detail. "Dad had a photographic memory," his son, Fred, recalls. "He actually participated in some military intelligence missions during the war in which he was transported to a location and then, upon return to base, was asked to reproduce the scene from memory." His paintings also drew upon Fred's knowledge of, and deep feeling for, the cowboys, horses, implements, landscape, and customs of the West. His lifelong affection for the Indians of his home area was especially well represented in his work. His serious art was further marked by the action, romance, and sense of humor which had enhanced the Red Ryder comic strip.

As it had with Red Ryder, the Fred Harman signature on artwork meant quality and a touch of something special that was uniquely Harman. Fred worked his canvases with no assistants. A perfectionist, he was at the same time prolific, completing up to 35 major works in a year. With a boost from his fame as the creator of Red Ryder, Fred quickly developed a reputation as one of the country's foremost Western artists, in the tradition of Charles M. Russell and Frederick Remington. Fred was honored by exhibits of his works at many prestigious galleries, including the National Cowboy Hall of Fame in Oklahoma City. His paintings have been reproduced in Western-oriented magazines such as Western Horseman, True West, and Westerner. Reproductions of 89 of his paintings, together with Fred's own colorful anecdotes on each, were compiled in a fine book, THE GREAT WEST IN PAINTINGS, published in 1969 by Swallow Press. Today, a Fred Harman original oil painting may sell for as much as 65,000 dollars.

Fred Harman passed away in January, 1982, leaving a legacy

Jim Bannon was the screen's last Red Ryder.

of enduring Western artistry for our continuing pleasure. Just as the Red Ryder Ranch welcomed visitors in the 1940's, fans today are encouraged to visit the Fred Harman Art Museum, a non-profit entity. Located in "Red Ryder country," two miles west of Pagosa Springs, Colorado, on U.S. Highway 160, the museum is housed in a structure that was Fred Harman's home before he died. Fred's son, Fred Harman III, serves as curator. Representing Fred Harman well, the museum which opened in 1982, is small, unpretentious, and homey. The memory of the 60-year career of Fred Harman: cowboy, illustrator, cartoonist, and Western artist, as well as the memory of Red Ryder and Little Beaver, is enshrined at this museum.

From the exterior of the site, visitors can view a panorama of natural beauty which give one an appreciation for Fred Harman's affection for the area. At the museum's entrance, visitors are greeted by a 5-foot high wood carving of Red Ryder and Little Beaver. The sculpture was a gift created for Fred's 72nd birthday. Inside, the walls are adorned with Harman paintings. There is a bronze bust of Fred Harman and various memorabilia of the Red Ryder years. On display are photos autographed by cowboy stars Fred counted as friends, including Bill Elliott, Gene Autry, Montie Montana, and the cast of television's "Gunsmoke."

In Fred's studio, appropriately, stand two easels, representing the major elements of his fame. One easel displays Red Ryder comic strip panels, and on the other an unfinished oil painting still stands where Fred left it before he died. On the studio walls are photographs of the cowboy actors who played Red Ryder, a photo of John Wayne visiting Fred at this home, and mementos of Fred's accomplishments. A collector's delight, studio shelves contain a full complement of Red Ryder Big Little Books and Whitman storybooks.

Fans may be interested to know that, in addition to the mu-

Allan Lane inherited the Ryder role after Bill Elliott.

seum, the Red Ryder legacy is still carried on today by rodeos named for the Fred Harman characters. In Pagosa Springs, the Red Ryder Rodeo is a Fourth of July tradition nearly 40 years old. About two weeks later in the year, the annual Little Beaver Rodeo, featuring Indian competition, is held in nearby

Dulce, New Mexico. At any time, visitors to the area can see Chimney Rock. Remember the Whitman storybook, RED RYDER AND THE ADVENTURE AT CHIMNEY ROCK?

In his lifetime, Fred Harman received many honors. He was chosen the first member of the board of directors of the Cow-

Elliott as Red Ryder and Bobby Blake as Little Beaver.

boy Artists of America. He was also a member of the National Cartoonists Society and the Society of Illustrators. In 1958, he was presented SERTOMA's "American Way of Life Award" as Colorado's Outstanding Citizen. But, Fred Harman was at heart a cowboy whose speech was as colorful as his artwork. As he was getting on in years, he described himself as, "An old cowhand who has smelled many smokefires."

Perhaps the dominant feature of Fred's life was his will to succeed. He credited his father with instilling his determination at a young age. Fred recalled his dad's advice to him not long after he had turned six. As Fred bounced in back of the saddle while clutching his dad's suspenders, his dad would yell, "Hang on, son!" Fred remembered those words throughout his life, particularly when times were discouraging.

On January 2,1982, at the age of 79, Fred Harman died of complications from a stroke suffered a week earlier. At his request, friends scattered his ashes on Square Top Mountain, not far from his home. Inspired by love of cowboys, Indians, horses, and the Western outdoors, he created comic strips and paintings that upheld the code of the West. Through his talent he achieved the true success that comes from touching the hearts of strangers and making them friends. Westerner magazine said it best, "His Red Ryder introduced the West to millions. His paintings have captured it for coming generations."

"You betchum, Red Ryder."

RONNIE AYCOTH—
BILL ELLIOTT LOOK-A-LIKE

During the past few years several people have shown up at the various film festivals dressed like their favorite cowboy star. One of the most impressive of these look-a-likes is Ronnie Aycoth, who impersonates Wild Bill Elliott when Elliott portrayed the screen's "Red Ryder." Aycoth, a native of Charlotte, North Carolina, bears a striking resemblance to the Western film star.

Ronnie started attending film conventions some 10 years ago

Honoring
the Memory of
"Wild Bill" Elliott

Ronnie
Aycoth
as
RED RYDER

and was told he looked a lot like Elliott. This gave him the idea of trying to put together a "Red Ryder" outfit. He contacted leathercrafter, Bob Brown, who had made the original holster and chaps for Elliott, and Brown agreed to make a similar rig for Aycoth. He then started to wear his newly-created attire to the film festivals. It caused an immediate stir among the fans, who often turned to get a second look at what seemed to be a reincarnation of Bill Elliott. Even Peggy Stewart, who worked with Elliott, was impressed and said, "Ronnie, you sure do bring back some wonderful memories."

Ronnie plans to attend many more film conventions and says of his hobby, "The best part of it all is the wonderful people I've met while attending Western events—friendships that are as dear as any that I have. It's been great fun and an encouragement to meet people who still have the old-time value system, as did our cowboy heroes that we idolized on the silver screen."

THE REAL WILD BILL vs. THE REEL WILD BILLS

contributed by Paul Dellinger

Picture this: "Wild Bill" Hickok, decked out in his fringed buckskins and fancy boots, is scouting on horseback, riding across the Western plains of 1871 with a hippie hairdo and a pair of sunglasses.

Which movie, you may be asking yourself, of the many which depicted Hickok, could that scene be from? According to Richard O'Connor's biography of WILD BILL HICKOK (1959, Doubleday and Co.), it's a scene out of Hickok's actual life.

In his later years, O'Connor tells us, Hickok had vision problems—rather a deadly disease for a gunfighter. The disease was diagnosed as ophthalmia, characterized by inflammation of the eyeballs. Hickok had to wear smoked glasses to curb the brightness that would dazzle him. Even he thought they looked ridiculous. He had no way of knowing dark glasses would one day become the style in Hollywood, the future home of many actors who would portray Hickok on the screen.

The drama of a Western lawman facing possible blindness would seem to offer many story possibilities—as, in fact, it has, but not in stories about Hickok. The exception was the 1923 silent movie production, WILD BILL HICKOK, with William S.

Hart in the role and Ethel Terry as "Calamity Jane." At the time, it was considered a fairly accurate account of Hickok's life story.

In many ways, Hickok's life was as interesting as some of the wilder myths of Wild Bill we have enjoyed in movies and TV.

Like Wyatt Earp and Bat Masterson, James Butler Hickok hailed from Illinois. After a brawl in which he mistakenly believed he had killed a man, he moved west where he fell in with none other than the famous scout, Kit Carson, who introduced him to the nocturnal saloon life he would come to enjoy.

There are two versions of how he came to be known as "Wild Bill", although the west was full of nicknames ranging from Mysterious Dave to Billy the Kid. His older brother, Lorenzo, somehow acquired the nickname "Billy Barnes" as a stage driver and freighter on the Santa Fe Trail, and the "Bill" part was said to have been transferred to the younger Hickok. The other account involves Hickok's coming to the defense of a bartender friend who had wounded an unruly customer, when a mob tried to take vengeance on the bartender.

It was in Independence, Missouri, that Hickok told the mob to disperse or "there'll be more dead men around here than the town can bury."

"Good for you, Wild Bill," a woman is said to have called as the mob broke up. She may have been the cheerleader that gave him his title.

One reason the mob broke up may have been the reputation Hickok had from the "McCanles massacre" of 1861. Some versions have Hickok downing 10 men in that affair, sustaining some 24 wounds himself. Actually, Hickok did shoot and kill Dave McCanles when he and two friends tried to throw Hickok's boss off some disputed stagecoach station property. Hickok

67p

666pppp6ppp6p67ppp66pp66pp6pp6666pppp666p66p66p66p6pp6pp6pp6p

appreciation for Hickok having acted as guide for a party of easterners who took a five-week tour of the wild west.

THE PLAINSMAN was remade in color in 1966, with Don Murray as Hickok (again with stag-handled pistols turned backwards), Abby Dalton, as a Calamity Jane many times more lovely than the real Martha Jane Canary, looked on her best day, and Guy Stockwell as an authoritative "Buffalo Bill". This version stopped short of Hickok being assassinated, and had the trio instead ride off into the sunset with the blessings of General George Armstrong Custer (Leslie Nielsen) after cleaning up a bit of gunrunning in Deadwood.

Both films had the scene, which the real William F. Cody recounted, of Hickok playing cards with a crooked gambler and pulling a gun when the gambler began raking in the chips. "I'm calling the hand that's in your hat," Hickok said, having seen the gambler getting rid of some cards that way.

In the DeMille version, Hickok is assassinated by Jack McCall, and sent heaven-ward (or somewhere) with a kiss from Calamity Jane. The implied romance—implied even more in the happier ending remake—appears to have been a tall story implied by the real Calamity Jane to increase her own stature after Hickok's death. She also is said to have claimed to have chased down McCall and captured him with a meat cleaver, but that account never happened, either, according to historians.

In FRONTIER SCOUT, George Houston's first Western, made in 1938, Houston played Hickok in something like the Cooper mold including the backwards guns. It was that same year that Columbia released a 15-chapter serial, THE GREAT ADVENTURES OF WILD BILL HICKOK, starring one Gordon Elliott.

From then on, Gordon Elliott would be better known as "Wild

Bill" Elliott, and the backwards stag-handled guns would be his movie trademark (along with his assertion, "I'm a peaceable man.")

The serial had Elliott-Hickok as marshal of Abilene, battling the "phantom raiders," to keep the Chisholm Trail open for cattle drives. Hickok did actually serve as marshal of Abilene, Kansas, from April to December, 1871. He was seemingly enticed by a winsome widow, Mrs. Agnes Thatcher Lake, who ran a circus, and was an accomplished horsewoman, animal trainer, and tightrope walker on her own. But when the feeling became mutual, Hickok shied away from the altar, going so far as to spread a story that he already had a wife back in Illinois to discourage her.

The Elliott version of Hickok was woman-shy, too, always riding away from the movie's heroine as "The End" flashed on the screen. But in Wyoming five years later, Hickok and Mrs. Lake crossed paths again—and were married the next day, on March 5, 1876. The movies have all shied away from that marriage, and, actually, the honeymoon lasted only two weeks before Hickok left for the Black Hills of Dakota with avowed intentions to seek a fortune in gold for his bride. Instead, he had an unforeseen date with Jack McCall, August 2, 1876, at age 39.

Elliott kept the "Wild Bill" tag, becoming "Wild Bill Saunders" in four Columbia films—THE TAMING OF THE WEST, PIONEERS OF THE FRONTIER, THE MAN FROM TUMBLEWEEDS, and THE RETURN OF WILD BILL. Then Columbia let him become Wild Bill Hickok again for a whole series of pictures in 1940 to 1942.

In PRAIRIE SCHOONERS, Hickok takes on land swindlers in Kansas. BEYOND THE SACRAMENTO pits him against confidence men in Lodestone. In ACROSS THE SIERRAS, Mitch Carew (Dick Curtis) tricks Hickok into killing a friend and Hickok, in chagrin, hangs up his guns—but takes them down again when Curtis returns for the customary last-reel shootout.

The real-life Hickok did once kill a friend by accident, and never had another gunfight. It was during those nine months as marshal of Abilene, when a gambler named Phil Coe tried to shoot Hickok and ended up face down instead. Mike Williams, a friend who was a special policeman at a local theater, came running out of the shadows with his pistol out, probably to help--but, seeing someone charging at him with a pistol, Hickok downed him, too. Perhaps it was his deteriorating eyesight, or the fact that his survival depended on shooting first and asking questions later. Hickok is said to have carried his friend's body into a saloon, placed it on a poker table, and wept over it—and then gone through the town in cold anger, closing up the saloons, and chasing the celebrating cowboys out.

The story was depicted on "Gunsmoke", with Matt Dillon, and Dodge City substituted for Hickok and Abilene—not only on TV with James Arness, but earlier on radio with William Conrad. (There was another "Gunsmoke" episode in which Will Bill Hickok is sent to arrest Marshal Dillon when Dillon is framed, but Dillon is able to prove his innocence and avoid a showdown with Hickok.)

In NORTH FROM THE LONE STAR, Hickok (Elliott) comes to Deadwood where the baddies mistakenly believe him to be on their side and make him marshal. Hickok never was marshal of Deadwood, where he ended his days, but it made a good story.

After doing Hickok again in HANDS ACROSS THE ROCKIES, helping sidekick Dub "Cannonball" Taylor track down his father's killer, Elliott was joined by Tex Ritter for KING OF DODGE CITY (which took place in Abilene, despite the title), ROARING FRONTIERS, THE LONE STAR VIGILANTES, BULLETS FOR

BANDITS (in which Elliott-Hickok meets an evil double, shoots
him, and then takes his place to save the ranch of his double's
mother), THE DEVIL'S TRAIL, and PRAIRIE GUNSMOKE.
(Elliott also played the sons of Daniel Boone, Davy Crockett,
and sported a mustache to play Mexican bandit Joaquin
Murietta during this period with Columbia.) Most of the scripts
have Hickok and Tex at odds in the beginning, and winding up
on the same side at the end.

Elliott dropped the Hickok role after that (although he did play
"Wild Bill Tolliver" in the serial THE VALLEY OF VANISHING
MEN) and, in 1943, moved over to Republic where he became
"Wild Bill Elliott" in a series of films, and later "Red Ryder,"
before moving up to higher-budgeted productions as "William
Elliott." He would again be billed as "Wild Bill Elliott", though
he would not play that role, in a series at Monogram-Allied
Artists from 1951 to 1954, and then make five movies playing
a modern day police lieutenant.

Meanwhile, the "Wild Bill Hickok" character was not lying dormant. Bruce Cabot played him in the 1942 production, WILD
BILL HICKOK RIDES, and did a good job at it. Even Roy Rogers
essayed the role in YOUNG BILL HICKOK in 1940, in between
movies where he also played romanticized versions of Jesse
James, Buffalo Bill, and Billy the Kid. Also in 1940, in the serial
DEADWOOD DICK, one of the characters is Hickok, as played
by Lane Chandler, in fancy coat and vest. Later, Richard Dix
and Robert Culp would even try on the role for size—Dix doing
it as a secondary character killed off early in the story, and
Culp as a sort of tongue-in-cheek version. Hickok is also a
character in Dustin Hoffman's LITTLE BIG MAN (1970).

The year 1953 was a varied one for Hickok. In PONY EX-
PRESS, Forrest Tucker plays him with the usual butt-forward
guns (only this time they are ivory, or pearl-handled) opposite
Charlton Heston's version of Buffalo Bill Cody. Pretty leading

ladies Rhonda Fleming and Jan Sterling brighten the color scenery, and Heston and Tucker engage in a lot of two-gun derring-do before the villains are brought to justice in the final reel, and California is united with the rest of the nation via Pony Express.

The first time you see "Hickok" and "Cody" together, they greet each other by standing in the street shooting, seeing how close each can come without hitting the other. "It's lots fancier than shakin' hands," Westerner Jan Sterling explains to easterner Rhonda Fleming.

In a considerably less expensively-filmed movie, SON OF THE RENEGADE, Hickok appears in a walk-on—this time with mustache and even a goatee along with his fancy clothes and stag-handled backwards pistols—to confront "Red River Johnny" Carpenter, or rather Johnny's father (Johnny Carpenter, as he was wont to do, played a dual role.) The elder Red River Johnny is a Robin Hood-type outlaw in the story, and Hickok warns him "you won't get away with it in my town, Red River." Then Hickok makes fun of the name: "That sounds like a man. But I don't think you're any part of a man."

"Careful, Johnny," warns the narrator who is telling the story of Johnny's father to start off the story. Hickok counts so they can shoot it out: "One . . . two . . . an ace!" he says, jerking out a derringer—perhaps the only time Hickok resorted to one on the screen, although he is said to have used them.

"You got a pair of sixes to beat, Bill," Carpenter says, getting his guns out just as fast.

"I guess we'll call this one a draw," Hickok decides wisely.

Hickok came off as the bad guy in JACK McCALL, DESPERADO, with hero George Montgomery as McCall and Douglas Kennedy as an evil Hickok. The story starts off with McCall walking into the saloon where Hickok is playing cards. Hickok goes for his gun—only one, this time - but Montgomery beats him, and is arrested. In his trial, he recounts the evil deeds Hickok performed, and is acquitted at the movie's end.

The real McCall—a somewhat less heroic figure than Montgomery—was also found innocent by a miners' court in Deadwood, even though he shot Hickok in the back. But he was later re-arrested, retried (his lawyer protested double jeopardy, but the court held that the first "trial" was not a legal one), and hanged McCall.

Carpenter would use the same idea in I KILLED WILD BILL HICKOK (1956), this time with Tom Brown playing Hickok as a meanie.

The other 1953 movie featuring Hickok was a musical titled CALAMITY JANE, with Doris Day playing her and singing such tunes as "My Secret Love" to Howard Keel's Hickok. It was light, pleasant, and only occasionally exciting, recounting the myth of the Hickok-Calamity Jane romance and giving it a happy ending.

Hickok had appeared briefly in THE LAWLESS BREED (1952), a whitewash of the John Wesley Hardin story with Rock Hudson and Julie Adams (previously seen in the Jimmy Stewart film BEND OF THE RIVER earlier that year). Legend has it that, during Hickok's brief marshaling at Abilene, Wes Hardin got the drop on him by pretending to hand over his gun and then spinning them back so that he had Hickok covered. The maneuver, known as the road agent's spin, was well known, however, and some historians doubt that Hickok would have been tricked by it.

In the movie, Hickok has disarmed Hardin (Hudson), and a

friend slips Hudson another pistol. Hudson covers Hickok, and tells him, for reasons integral to the plot, "I'm gonna need my gun, Marshal." He gets it, along with a warning to be out of town by a certain time or to use it. The time comes. Hickok bursts into the saloon and shoots a clock off the wall by way of drawing Hudson's attention to this, and Hudson meekly leaves town.

Wild Bill moved onto radio and TV in the 1950s with Guy Madison, accompanied by Andy Devine as his deputy-sidekick, Jingles. Madison, sporting the customary butt-forward stag handles, played Hickok as a perpetual lawman—and, on one occasion, had to thrash an opponent played by none other than Johnny Carpenter.

The death toll attributed to Hickok's guns in legend comes near that accumulated in the TV series or all those gunned down in the Elliott version of Hickok. The actual number seems to have been only 17, with all but three of the gunfights occurring when Hickok was serving as a lawman. That number does not count his casualties during the Civil War or in Indian fighting.

His legend may have started in the eastern magazines when he became a drinking buddy of Henry M. Stanley (who would one day go on to find Dr. Livingston who was lost in Africa, and gain fame from the quotation: "Dr. Livingston, I presume"). It happened at Fort Riley, Kansas, where Hickok was working as a deputy marshal hired to bring back deserters and the horses and supplies they stole, and Stanley was a correspondent for the New York Herald. Other writers jumped on the bandwagon.

While a scout, Hickok became friendly with Lt. Col. Custer and Custer's wife, and was a frequent guest in their home. Custer and Hickok had much in common, from their flamboyance to their long hair - and their deaths which occurred the same year, 1876.

Hickok tried to take advantage of his fame with a touring show featuring four Comanches, several buffalo (which he and his friends got aboard a train after much difficulty), and himself. "The Daring Buffalo Chase of the Plains" played for one performance, at Niagara Falls in 1870. It folded when the buffalo got loose, and caused some havoc in the community.

Buffalo Bill still managed to persuade Hickok to join another show three years later, scripted by Ned Buntline whose tall tales had brought Cody no small measure of fame back east. Hickok was willing to take the money, but could not bring himself to utter such lines as: "Fear not, fair maid. By heavens, you are safe at last with Wild Bill, who is ever ready to risk his life and die, if need be, in defense of weak and defenseless womanhood." Elliott and others got much better lines.

During one sequence when Hickok and Cody were supposed to be sitting around a campfire drinking whiskey, Hickok complained during a performance that he was only getting cold tea, and refused to continue until he was supplied with the real thing. Cody later said he was afraid the show had been ruined, but that the audience liked it, and Wild Bill got his whiskey for the scene therefter.

He did tend to become a bit more amorous with the heroine than the script called for, and he also had a tendency to make the supposedly-dead Indians lying on stage jump by shooting blanks at their legs and burning them.

He disliked the stage so much that he would try to hide behind the scenery while calling out his lines, but the technician handling the lighting would illuminate him everytime. Until, that is, an exasperated Hickok took one of his pistols, and hurled it through the light.

He finally quit the tour, but returned as part of the audience in

New York when he heard an actor had been hired to play him. The actor did such a bad job, in Hickok's view, that he felt called upon to return to the stage, and manhandle the actor through his paces. The incident led to his arrest, briefly.

However, it is probably safe to say that the depiction of Hickok was better left to Gary Cooper, Bill Elliott, Guy Madison, and all the others who did the job. Hickok himself would not have enjoyed acting.

THE NON-STARRING FILMS OF BILL ELLIOTT

1925 The Plastic Age - Clara Bow, Gilbert Roland
1926 Napoleon, Jr. - Jerry Madden, Frank Coleman
1927 The Drop Kick - Richard Barthelmess, Dorothy Revier
 The Private Life of Helen of Troy - Richard Cortez, Lewis
  Stone
1928 The Valley of Hunted Men - Buffalo Bill, Jr.
 Arizona Wildcat - Tom Mix
 Beyond London's Lights
1929 Restless Youth - Marceline Day, Ralph Forbes
 Passion Song - Noah Beery, Gertrude Olmstead
 Broadway Scandals - Carmel Myers, Sally O'Neill
1930 She Couldn't Say No - Winnie Lightner, Chester Morris
 The Great Divide - Dorothy Mackaill, Ian Keith
 Sunny - Marilyn Miller, Lawrence Gray
 The Midnight Mystery - Betty Compson, Lowell Sherman
1931 City Streets - Gary Cooper, Sylvia Sidney
 God's Gift to Women - Frank Fay, Laura La Plante
 Born to Love - Constance Bennett, Joel McCrea
 Palmy Days - Eddie Cantor, Charlotte Greenwood
 Convicted - Allen Pringle, Jameson Thomas
 Delicious - Janet Gaynor, Charles Farrell
 Night After Night - George Raft, Constance Cummings
1932 One Hour with You - Maurice Chevalier, Jeanette
  MacDonald
 Vanity Fair - Myrna Loy, Conway Tearle

The Rich are Always with Us - Ruth Chatterton, George Brent

The Jewel Robbery - William Powell, Kay Francis

Crooner - David Manners, Ann Dvorak

Merrily We Go to Hell - Sylvia Sidney, Fredric March

Lady with a Past - Constance Bennett, Ben Lyon

1933 Peg O' My Heart - Marion Davies, Onslow Stevens

The Little Giant - Edward G. Robinson, Mary Astor

Gold Diggers of 1933 - Warren William, Joan Blondell

Private Detective - William Powell, Margaret Lindsay

The Keyhole - Kay Francis, George Brent

1934 20 Million Sweethearts - Dick Powell, Pat O'Brien

The Case of the Howling Dog - Warren William, Mary Astor

Here Comes the Navy - James Cagney, Pat O'Brien

Wonder Bar - Al Jolson, Dolores Del Rio

Registered Nurse - Bebe Daniels, John Halliday

A Modern Hero - Richard Barthelmess, Jean Muir

1935 Secret Bride - Barbara Stanwyck, Warren William

Devil Dogs of the Air - James Cagney, Pat O'Brien

Gold Diggers of 1935 - Dick Powell, Gloria Stuart

Go Into Your Dance - Al Jolson, Ruby Keeler

The Woman in Red - Barbara Stanwyck, Gene Raymond

The Traveling Saleslady - Joan Blondell, Glenda Farrell

G-Men - James Cagney, Ann Dvorak

A Night At the Ritz - William Gargan, Patricia Ellis

The Girl From 10th Avenue - Bette Davis, Ian Hunter

Alibi Ike - Joe E. Brown, Olivia DeHavilland

Broadway Gondolier - Dick Powell, Joan Blondell

Bright Lights - Joe E. Brown, Ann Dvorak

The Goose and the Gander - Kay Francis, George Brent

Broadway Hostess - Wini Shaw, Phil Regan

Dr. Socrates - Paul Muni, Ann Dvorak

I Live for Love - Dolores Del Rio, Everett Marshall

Stars Over Broadway - James Melton, Jane Froman

The Story of Louis Pasteur - Paul Muni, Josephine

Hutchinson
Dangerous - Bette Davis, Franchot Tone
Ceiling Zero - James Cagney, Pat O'Brien
Moonlight on the Prairie - Dick Foran, Sheila Mannors
While the Patient Slept - Aline McMahon, Guy Kibbee
1936 The Murder of Dr. Harrigan - Ricardo Cortez, Mary Astor
The Singing Kid - Al Jolson, Sybil Jason
The Big Noise - Guy Kibbee, Warren Hull
Two Against the World - Humphrey Bogart, Beverly Roberts
Bullets or Ballots - Edward G. Robinson, Joan Blondell
Murder by an Aristocrat - Lyle Talbot, Marguerite Churchill
Polo Joe - Joe E. Brown, Carol Hughes
Trailin' West - Dick Foran, Paula Stone
Down the Stretch - Mickey Rooney, Patricia Ellis
The Case of the Black Cat - Ricardo Cortez, Jane Bryan
The Case of the Velvet Claw - Warren William, Claire Dodd
Romance In the Air - Wini Shaw, Phil Regan
1937 Guns of the Pecos - Dick Foran, Anne Nagel
Fugitive in the Sky - Jean Muir, Warren Hull
Melody for Two - James Melton, Patricia Ellis
Midnight Court - Ann Dvorak, John Litel
Speed to Spare - Charles Quigley, Dorothy Wilson
You Can't Have Everything - Alice Faye, Don Ameche
Love Takes Flight - Bruce Cabot, Beatrice Roberts
Wife, Doctor and Nurse - Loretta Young, Warner Baxter
Boots and Saddles - Gene Autry, Smiley Burnette
The Walking Dead - Boris Karloff, Edmund Gwen
Swing It, Professor - Pinky Tomlin, Paula Stone
Boy of the Streets - Jackie Cooper, Maureen O'Connor
Roll Along Cowboy - Smith Ballew, Cecilia Parker
1938 Lady In the Morgue - Preston Foster, Patricia Ellis
The Devil's Party - Victor McLaglen, William Gargan
Tarzan's Revenge - Glenn Morris, Eleanor Holm

THE STARRING FILMS
OF BILL ELLIOTT

The Great Adventures of Wild Bill Hickok: (15 chapter serial) Columbia 1938. Gordon Elliott, Monte Blue, Frankie Darro, Dickie Jones, Sammy McKim, Kermit Maynard, Chief Thundercloud, Mala, Roscoe Ates, Monte Collins, Carol Wayne, J. P. McGowan, Eddy Waller, Walter Wills, Reed Hadley, Lee Phelps, Robert Fiske, Earle Hodgins, Ed Brady, Earl Dwire, Edmund Cobb, Art Mix, Slim Whitaker, George Chesebro, Alan Bridge, Ray Jones, Hal Taliaferro, Blackie Whiteford, Walter Miller.
Director: Mack V. Wright.

In Early Arizona: Columbia 1938. 53 minutes. Gordon (Bill) Elliott, Dorothy Gulliver, Harry Woods, Franklyn Farnum, Art Davis, Charles King, Ed Cassidy, Jack Ingram, Slim Whitaker, Bud Osborne, Lester Dorr, Symona Boniface, Buzz Barton, Tom London, Dick Dorrell, Oscar Gahan, Jess Cavan, Kit Guard, Frank Ellis, Al Ferguson, Frank Ball, Tex Palmer, Jack O'Shea, Sherry Tansey.
Director: Joseph Levering.

Frontiers of '49: Columbia 1939. 54 minutes. Bill Elliott, Luana de Alcaniz, Charles King, Hal Taliaferro, Slim Whitaker, Octavio Giraud, Carlos Villarias, Joe de la Cruz, Jack Walters, Al Ferguson, Bud Osborne, Kit Guard, Jack Ingram, Lee Shumway, Ed Cassidy, Tex Palmer.

Director: Joseph Levering.

Lone Star Pioneers: Columbia 1939. 56 minutes. Bill Elliott, Dorothy Gulliver, Lee Shumway, Slim Whitaker, Charles King, Jack Ingram, Harry Harvey, Buzz Barton, Frank LaRue, Budd Buster, Dave Sharpe, Frank Ellis, Kit Guard, Merrill McCormack, Jack Rockwell, Tex Palmer.
Director: Joseph Levering.

The Law Comes to Texas: Columbia 1939. 58 minutes. Bill Elliott, Veda Ann Borg, Bud Osborne, Slim Whitaker, Leon Beaumont, Paul Everton, Charles King, Lee Shumway, Jack LaRue, Edmund Cobb, Frank Ellis, David Sharpe, Forrest Taylor, Lane Chandler, Budd Buster, Dan White, Ben Corbett.

You can bet Frank Ellis won't get away with Wild Bill's shooting iron in this scene from THE LAW COMES TO TEXAS.

Overland with Kit Carson: (15 chapter serial) Columbia 1939. Bill Elliott, Iris Meredith, Richard Fiske, Bobby Clack, Trevor Bardette, LeRoy Mason, Olin Francis, James Craig, Francis Sayles, Kenneth MacDonald, Dick Curtis, Richard

Bill Elliott with perennial Western heroine Iris Meredith, in the serial OVERLAND WITH KIT CARSON (Columbia, 1939).

Botiller, Hal Taliaferro, Ernie Adams, Flo Campbell, John Tyrrell, Francisco Moran, Hank Bell, Irene Herndon, Art Mix, Jack Rockwell, Iron Eyes Cody, Martin Garralaga, Del Lawrence, Bobby Clack, J. W. Cody, Lee Prather, Robert Fiske, Edward LeSaint, Carl Stockdale, Joe Garcia, Stanley Brown, Eddie Foster.
Directors: Sam Nelson and Norman Deming.

The Taming of the West: Columbia 1939. 55 minutes. Bill Elliott, Dub Taylor, Iris Meridith, Dick Curtis, James Craig, Stanley Brown, Ethan Allen, Kenneth MacDonald, Victor Wong, Charles King, Don Beddoe, Lane Chandler, Art Mix, Richard Fiske, John Tyrrell, Bob Woodward, Hank Bell, Irene Herndon, Jack Kirk, George Morrell.
Director: Norman Deming.

Pioneers of the Frontier: Columbia 1940. 58 minutes. Bill

Dick Curtis gets beat up again in TAMING OF THE WEST.

Elliott, Dub Taylor, Linda Winters, Dick Curtis, Stanley Brown, Richard Fiske, Carl Stockdale, Lafe McKee, Ralph McCullough, Al Bridge, Edmund Cobb, George Chesebro, Lynton Brent, Jack Kirk, Ralph Peters.
Director: Sam Nelson.

The Man From Tumbleweeds: Columbia 1940. 59 minutes. Bill Elliott, Dub Taylor, Iris Meredith, Raphael "Ray" Bennett, Francis Walker, Ernie Adams, Al Hill, Stanley Brown, Richard Fiske, Edward LeSaint, Don Beddoe, Eddie Laughton, John Tyrrell, Ed Cecil, Jack Lowe, Buel Bryant, Olin Francis, Jay Lawrence, Bruce Bennett (Herman Brix), George Chesebro, Hank Bell, Steve Clark, Ray Jones.
Director: Joseph H. Lewis.

The Return of Wild Bill: Columbia 1940. 60 minutes. Bill

Bill Elliott gets a grip on Richard Fiske in THE MAN FROM TUMBLEWEEDS.

Elliott, Dub Taylor, Iris Meredith, Luana Walters, George Lloyd, Ed LeSaint, Frank LaRue, Francis Walker, Chuck Morrison, Buel Bryant, William Kellogg, Jack Rockwell, Jim Corey, John Ince, Tex Cooper.
Director: Joseph H. Lewis.

Prairie Schooners: Columbia 1940. 58 minutes. Bill Elliott, Dub Taylor, Evelyn Young, Kenneth Harlan, Ray Teal, Bob Burns, Netta Parker, Richard Fiske, Edmund Cobb, Jim Thorpe, Sammy Stein, Ned Glass, Lucien Maxwell, George Morrell, Merrill McCormack.
Director: Sam Nelson.

Beyond the Sacramento: Columbia 1940. 58 minutes. Bill Elliott, Dub Taylor, Evelyn Keyes, John Dilson, Bradley Page, Frank LaRue, Norman Willis, Steve Clark, Jack Clifford, Don Beddoe, Harry Bailey, Art Mix, Bud Osborne, Blackjack Ward, George McKay, Jack Clifford, Olin Francis, Clem Horton, Tex Cooper, Ned Glass.
Director: Lambert Hillyer.

The Wildcat of Tucson: Columbia 1940. 58 minutes. Bill Elliott, Dub Taylor, Evelyn Young, Stanley Brown, Kenneth MacDonald, Ben Taggart, Edmund Cobb, George Lloyd, Sammy Stein, Francis Walker, Robert Winkler, Forrest Taylor, Dorothy Andre, Bert Young, Newt Kirby, Johnny Daheim, Murdock McQuarrie.
Director: Lambert Hillyer.

Across the Sierras: Columbia 1941. 58 minutes. Bill Elliott, Dub Taylor, Richard Fiske, Luana Walters, Dick Curtis, LeRoy Mason, Ruth Robinson, John Dilson, Milt Kibbee, Ralph Peters, Eddie Laughton, Carl Knowles, Tom London, Jim Pierce, Edmund Cobb, Art Mix, Ed Coxen, Tex Cooper.
Director: Ross Lederman.

It may be music to Dub "Cannonball" Taylor and Tex Cooper, but not to Wild Bill's ears, in this scene from ACROSS THE SIERRAS.

North From the Lone Star: Columbia 1941. 58 minutes. Bill Elliott, Dub Taylor, Dorothy Fay, Richard Fiske, Arthur Loft, Jack Roper, Chuck Morrison, Claire Rochelle, Al Rhein, Edmund Cobb, Steve Clark, Art Mix, Hank Bell, Dick Botiller. Director: Lambert Hillyer.

The Return of Daniel Boone: Columbia 1941. 60 minutes. Bill Elliott, Dub Taylor, Betty Miles, Ray Bennett, Walter Soderling, Carl Stockdale, Bud Osborne, Roy Butler, , Art Miles, Edwin Bryant, Steve Clark, Murdock MacQuarrie, Hank Bell, Francis Walker, Tom Carter. Director: Lambert Hillyer.

Hands Across the Rockies: Columbia 1941. 58 minutes. Bill Elliott, Dub Taylor, Mary Daily, Kenneth MacDonald,

Frank LaRue, Donald Curtis, Tom Moray, Stanley Brown, Slim Whitaker, Harrison Greene, Art Mix, Eddy Waller, Hugh Prosser, Edmund Cobb, John Tyrrell, George Morrell, Kathryn Bates, Eddie Laughton, Ethan Laidlaw, Buck Moulton.
Director: Lambert Hillyer.

The Son of Davy Crockett: Columbia 1941. 59 minutes. Bill Elliott, Dub Taylor, Iris Meredith, Kenneth MacDonald, Richard Fiske, Eddy Waller, Don Curtis, Paul Scanlon, Edmund Cobb, Steve Clark, Harrison Greene, Lloyd Bridges, Stanley Brwon, Eddie Laughton, Martin Garralaga, Francis Sayles, Dick Botiller, Jack Ingram, Frank LaRue, John Tyrrell, Russ Powell, Tom London, Chuck Hamilton, Sven Borg, Curley Dresden, Frank Ellis, Merrill McCormack, Ray Jones, Lew Meehan.
Director: Lambert Hillyer.

King of Dodge City: Columbia 1941. 63 minutes. Bill Elliott, Tex Ritter, Dub Taylor, Guy Usher, Judith Linden, Rick Anderson, Kenneth Harlan, Pierce Lyden, Francis Walker, Harrison Greene, Jack Rockwell, Russ Powell, Frosty Royce, Jack Ingram, Ed Coxen, Lee Prather, Tris Coffin, Ed Cobb, Jay Lawrence, Ned Glass, George Morrell, George Chesebro, Steve Clark, Horace B. Carpenter, Ted Mapes.
Director: Lambert Hillyer.

Roaring Frontiers: Columbia 1941. 62 minutes. Bill Elliott, Tex Ritter, Frank Mitchell, Ruth Ford, Bradley Page, Tris Coffin, Hal Taliaferro, Francis Walker, Joe McGuinn, George Chesebro, Charles Stevens, Charles King, Lew Meehan, Hank Bell, George Eldredge, Fred Burns, Ernie Adams.
Director: Lambert Hillyer.

The Lone Star Vigilantes: Columbia 1942. 58 minutes. Bill Elliott, Tex Ritter, Frank Mitchell, Virginia Carpenter, Luana

Bill Elliott and Tex Ritter in a scene from the Columbia production THE ROARING FRONTIERS.

Walters, Budd Buster, Forrest Taylor, Gavin Gordon, Lowell Drew, Ed Cobb, Ethan Laidlaw, Rick Anderson.
Director: Wallace Fox.

Bullets for Bandits: Columbia 1942. 55 minutes. Bill Elliott, Tex Ritter, Frank Mitchell, Dorothy Short, Ralph Theodore, Forrest Taylor, Edythe Elliott, Eddie Laughton, Joe McGunn, Tom Moray, Art Mix, Harry Harvey, Hal Taliaferro, John Tyrrell, Bud Osborne.
Director: Wallace Fox.

North of the Rockies: Columbia 1942. 60 minutes. Bill Elliott, Tex Ritter, Frank Mitchell, Shirley Patterson, Larry Parks, John Miljan, Ian MacDonald, Lloyd Bridges, Gertrude Hoffman, Earl Gunn, Boyd Irwin, Art Dillard, David Harper,

Francis Sayles.
Director: Lambert Hillyer.

The Devil's Trail: Columbia 1942. 61 minutes. Bill Elliott, Tex Ritter, Frank Mitchell, Eileen O'Hearn, Noah Beery, Ruth Ford, Art Mix, Joel Friedkin, Joe McGuinn, Ed Cobb, Tris Coffin, Paul Newland, Steve Clark, Sarah Padden, Bud Osborne, Stanley Brown, Buck Moulton.
Director: Lambert Hillyer.

Prairie Gunmoke: Columbia 1942. 56 minutes. Bill Elliott, Tex Ritter, Frank Mitchell, Hal Price, Tris Coffin, Joe McGuinn, Frosty Royce, Rich Anderson, Art Mix, Francis Walker, Ray Jones, Ted Mapes, Glenn Strange, Steve Clark.
Director: Lambert Hillyer.

Vengeance of the West: Columbia 1942. 60 minutes. Bill Elliott, Tex Ritter, Frank Mitchell, Dick Curtis, Richard Fiske, Ted Mapes, Eva Pulig, Jose Tortosa, Guy Wilkerson, Ed Cobb, Eddie Laughton, Stanley Brown, John Tyrrell, Steve Clark.
Director: Lambert Hillyer.

The Valley of Vanishing Men: (15 chapter serial) Columbia 1942. Bill Elliott, Slim Summerfield, Carmen Morales, Kenneth MacDonald, Jack Ingram, George Chesebro, John Shay, Tom London, Arno Frey, Julian Rivero, Roy Barcroft, I. Stanford Jolley, Ted Mapes, Lane Chandler, Ernie Adams, Michael Vallon, Robert Fiske, Davidson Clark, Lane Bradford, Chief Thundercloud, Blackie Whiteford.
Director: Spencer Gordon Bennet.

Calling Wild Bill Elliott: Republic 1943. 54 minutes. Wild Bill Elliott, George "Gabby" Hayes, Anne Jeffreys, Buzz Henry, Fred Kohler, Jr., Roy Barcroft, Herbert Heyes, Charles King, Frank Hagney, Bud Geary, Lynton Brent, Frank

McCarroll, Burr Caruth, Forbes Murray, Ted Mapes, Herman Hack, Yakima Canutt.
Director: Spencer Gordon Bennet.

The Man From Thunder River: Republic 1943. 59 minutes. Wild Bill Elliott, George "Gabby" Hayes, Anne Jeffreys, Ian Keith, John James, Georgia Cooper, Jack Ingram, Eddie Lee, Charles King, Bud Geary, Jack Rockwell, Ed Cassidy, Roy Brent, Alan Bridge, Al Taylor, Ed Cobb, Robert Barron, Jack O'Shea, Curley Dresden, Frank McCarroll.
Director: John English.

Bordertown Gun Fighters: Republic 1943. 55 minutes. Wild Bill Elliott, George "Gabby" Hayes, Anne Jeffreys, Ian Keith, Harry Woods, Roy Barcroft, Bud Geary, Karl Hackett, Charles King, Carl Sepulveda, Edward Keane, Frank McCarroll, Wheaton Chambers, Ken Terrell, Neal Hart, Frosty Royce, Marshall Reed, Bill Wolfe.
Director: Howard Bretherton.

Wagon Tracks West: Republic 1943. 55 minutes. Wild Bill Elliott, George "Gabby" Hayes, Anne Jeffreys, Tom Tyler, Rick Vallin, Robert Frazer, Roy Barcroft, Charles Miller, Tom London, Cliff Lyons, Jack Rockwell, Kenne Duncan, Minerva Urecal, Hal Price, Frank Ellis, Hank Bell, William Nestell, Jack Ingram, Jack O'Shea, Ray Jones, Curley Dresden, Frank McCarroll, Marshall Reed, Ben Corbett, Jack Montgomery, Tom Steele, Roy Butler.
Director: Howard Bretherton.

Death Valley Manhunt: Republic 1943. 55 minutes. Wild Bill Elliott, George "Gabby" Hayes, Anne Jeffreys, Weldon Heyburn, Herbert Heyes, Davidson Clark, Pierce Lyden, Jack Kirk, Bud Geary, Marshall Reed, Charles Murray, Jr., Edward Keane, Curley Dresden.
Director: John English.

Anne Jeffreys, dressed as an Indian squaw, asks her leading man, Wild Bill Elliott, to try on an Indian headdress during a break in filming WAGON TRACKS WEST.

Overland Mail Robbery: Republic 1943. 55 minutes. Wild Bill Elliott, George "Gabby" Hayes, Anne Jeffreys, Weldon Heyburn, Nancy Gay, Kirk Alyn, Roy Barcroft, Bud Geary, Tom London, Alice Fleming, Jack Kirk, Kenne Duncan, Jack

Rockwell, Frank McCarroll, Jack O'Shea, LeRoy Mason, Hank Bell, Cactus Mack, Ray Jones, Tom Steele, Frank Ellis, Maxine Doyle.
Director: John English.

Mojave Firebrand: Republic 1944. 55 minutes. Wild Bill Elliott, George "Gabby" Hayes, Anne Jeffreys, LeRoy Mason, Jack Ingram, Harry McKim, Karl Hackett, Forrest Taylor, Hal Price, Marshall Reed, Kenne Duncan, Bud Geary, Jack Kirk, Fred Graham, Tom London, Frank Ellis, Tom Steele, Bob Burns, Art Dillard, Bud Osborne.
Director: Spencer Gordon Bennet.

Hidden Valley Outlaws: Republic 1944. 55 minutes. Wild Bill Elliott, George "Gabby" Hayes, Anne Jeffreys, Roy Barcroft, Kenne Duncan, John James, Charles Miller, Budd Buster, Tom London, LeRoy Mason, Earle Hodgins, Yakima Canutt, Fred "Snowflake" Toones, Jack Kirk, Tom Steele, Bud Geary, Frank McCarroll, Ed Cassidy, Robert Wilke, Cactus Mack, Forbes Murray, Frank O'Connor.
Director: Howard Bretherton.

Tucson Raiders: (Red Ryder) Republic 1944. 55 minutes. Wild Bill Elliott, Bobby Blake, George "Gabby" Hayes, Alice Fleming, Peggy Stewart, LeRoy Mason, Ruth Lee, Stanley Andrews, John Whitney, Bud Geary, Karl Hackett, Tom Steele, Tom Chatterton, Ed Cassidy, Fred Graham, Frank McCarroll, Marshall Reed.
Director: Spencer Gordon Bennet.

Marshal of Reno: (Red Ryder) Republic 1944. 54 minutes. Wild Bill Elliott, Bobby Blake, George "Gabby" Hayes, Alice Fleming, Herbert Rawlinson, Jay Kirby, Tom London, Kenne Duncan, Charles King, Jack Kirk, LeRoy Mason, Robert Wilke, Fred Burns, Tom Steele, Ed Cobb, Fred Graham, Blake Edwards, Hal Price, Bud Geary, Jack O'Shea, Al Tay-

lor, Marshall Reed, Tom Chatterton, Carl Sepulveda, Kenneth Terrell, Horace B. Carpenter, Charles Sullivan, Roy Barcroft.
Director: Wallace Grissell.

The San Antonio Kid: (Red Ryder) Republic 1944. 59 minutes. Wild Bill Elliott, Bobby Blake, Alice Fleming, Linda Stirling, Tom London, Earle Hodgins, Glenn Strange, Duncan Renaldo, LeRoy Mason, Jack Kirk, Robert Wilke, Jack O'Shea, Tex Terry, Bob Woodward, Herman Hack, Henry Wills, Tom Steele, Billy Vincent, Bud Geary, Cliff Parkinson.
Director: Howard Bretherton.

Cheyenne Wildcat: (Red Ryder) Republic 1944. 56 minutes. Wild Bill Elliott, Bobby Blake, Alice Fleming, Peggy Stewart, Francis McDonald, Roy Barcroft, Kenne Duncan, Bud Geary, Jack Kirk, Bud Osborne, Robert Wilke, Rex Lease, Tom Steele, Forrest Taylor, Franklyn Farnum, Horace B. Carpenter, Frank Ellis, Steve Clark, Bob Burns, Jack O'Shea.
Director: Lesley Selander.

Vigilantes of Dodge City: (Red Ryder) Republic 1944. 54 minutes. Wild Bill Elliott, Bobby Blake, Alice Fleming, Linda Stirling, LeRoy Mason, Tom London, Hal Taliaferro, Kenne Duncan, Bud Geary, Stephen Barclay, Robert Wilke, Stanley Andrews, Horace B. Carpenter.
Director: Wallace Grissell.

Sheriff of Las Vegas: (Red Ryder) Republic 1944. 55 minutes. Wild Bill Elliott, Bobby Blake, Alice Fleming, Peggy Stewart, Selmer Jackson, William Haade, Jay Kirby, John Hamilton, Kenne Duncan, Bud Geary, Jack Kirk, Frank McCarroll.
Director: Lesley Selander.

Bill with Tom London in VIGILANTES OF DODGE CITY (Republic, 1944).

Great Stagecoach Robbery: (Red Ryder) Republic 1945. 55 minutes. Wild Bill Elliott, Bobby Blake, Alice Fleming, Francis McDonald, Don Costello, Sylvia Arslan, Bud Geary, Leon Tyler, Henry Wills, Hank Bell, Robert Wilke, John James, Tom London. Horace B. Carpenter, Grace Cunard, Freddie Chapman.
Director: Lesley Selander.

Lone Texas Ranger: (Red Ryder) Republic 1945. 56 minutes. Wild Bill Elliott, Bobby Blake, Alice Fleming, Roy Barcroft, Helen Talbot, Jack McClendon, Rex Lease, Tom Chatterton, Jack Kirk, Nelson McDowell, Dale Van Sickel, Frank O'Connor, Robert Wilke, Bud Geary, Budd Buster, Hal Price, Horace B. Carpenter, Nolan Leary, Tom Steele, LeRoy Mason.
Director: Spencer Gordon Bennet.

Bells of Rosarita: Republic 1945. 68 minutes. Roy Rogers, Dale Evans, George "Gabby" Hayes, Bob Nolan and the Sons of the Pioneers, Grant Withers, Adele Mara, Roy Barcroft, Earle Hodgins, Addison Richards, Janet Martin, Syd Saylor, Ed Cassidy, Kenne Duncan, Rex Lease, Robert Wilke, Ted Mapes, Wally West, The Robert Mitchell Boy Choir, Helen Talbot, Poodles Hanneford, Hank Bell, Eddie Kane, Tom London, Marin Saris, Sam Ash, Barbara Elliott, Mary McCarty; Guest stars: Wild Bill Elliott, Allan Lane, Robert Livingston, Don "Red" Barry, Sunset Carson. Director: Frank McDonald.

Phantom of the Plains: (Red Ryder) Republic 1945. 56 minutes. Wild Bill Elliott, Bobby Blake, Alice Fleming, Ian Keith, William Haade, Virginia Christine, Jack Rockwell, Tom London, Earle Hodgins, Bud Geary, Henry Hall, Fred Graham, Jack Kirk, Rose Plummer. Director: Lesley Selander.

Marshal of Laredo: (Red Ryder) Republic 1945. 56 minutes. Wild Bill Elliott, Bobby Blake, Alice Fleming, Peggy Stewart, Roy Barcroft, Tom London, George Carlton, Wheaton Chambers, Tom Chatterton, George Chesebro, Don Costello, Bud Geary, Sarah Padden, Jack O'Shea, Lane Bradford, Kenneth Terrell, Dorothy Granger. Director: R. G. Springsteen.

Colorado Pioneers: (Red Ryder) Republic 1945. 55 minutes. Wild Bill Elliott, Bobby Blake, Alice Fleming, Roy Barcroft, Bud Geary, Billy Cummings, Freddie Chapman, Frank Jaquet, Tom London, Monte Hale, Buckwheat Thomas, George Chesebro, Emmett Vogan, Tom Chatterton, Ed Cassidy, Fred Graham, Horace B. Carpenter, Bill Wolfe, Jack Rockwell, George Morrell, Jack Kirk. Director: R. G. Springsteen.

"Now be careful, Red," says pretty Peggy Stewart as Alice "Duchess" Fleming looks on in this scene from MARSHAL OF LAREDO.

Wagon Wheels Westward: (Red Ryder) Republic 1945. 55 minutes. Wild Bill Elliott, Bobby Blake, Alice Fleming, Emmett Lynn, Linda Stirling, Roy Barcroft, Jay Kirby, Dick Curtis, George J. Lewis, Bud Geary, Tom London, Kenne Duncan, George Chesebro, Tom Chatterton, Frank Ellis, Bob McKenzie, Jack Kirk.
Director: R. G. Springsteen.

California Gold Rush: (Red Ryder) Republic 1946. 56 minutes. Wild Bill Elliott, Bobby Blake, Alice Fleming, Peggy Stewart, Russell Simpson, Dick Curtis, Kenne Duncan, Monte Hale, Tom London, Joel Friedkin, Wen Wright, Jack Kirk, Budd Buster, Bud Osborne, Neal Hart, Frank Ellis, Herman Hack, Dickie Dillon.
Director: R. G. Springsteen.

Sheriff of Redwood Valley: (Red Ryder) Republic 1946. 54 minutes. Wild Bill Elliott, Bobby Blake, Bob Steele, Peggy Stewart, Arthur Loft, James Craven, Tom London, Kenne Duncan, Bud Geary, Tom Chatterton, Bud Osborne, Frank McCarroll. Director: R. G. Springsteen.

Sun Valley Cyclone: (Red Ryder) Republic 1946. 56 minutes. Wild Bill Elliott, Bobby Blake, Alice Fleming, Roy Barcroft, Monte Hale, Kenne Duncan, Eddy Waller, Tom London, Ed Cobb, Ed Cassidy, George Chesebro, Rex Lease, Hal Price, Jack Kirk, Frank O'Connor, Jack Sparks. Director: R. G. Springsteen.

In Old Sacramento: Republic 1946. 89 minutes. William Elliott, Constance Moore, Hank Daniels, Ruth Donnelly, Eugene Pallette, Lionel Stander, Jack LaRue, Grant Withers, Bobby Blake, Charles Judels, Paul Hurst, Victoria Horne, Dick Wessel, Hal Taliaferro, Jack O'Shea, Marshall Reed, Eddy Waller, William Haade, Boyd Irwin, Lucien Littlefield, Ethel Wales, William B. Davidson, Ellen Corby, Fred Burns, Elaine Lange. Director: Joseph Kane.

Conquest of Cheyenne: (Red Ryder) Republic 1946. 55 minutes. Wild Bill Elliott, Bobby Blake, Alice Fleming, Peggy Stewart, Jay Kirby, Milton Kibbee, Tom London, Emmett Lynn, Kenne Duncan, George Sherwood, Frank McCarroll, Jack Kirk, Tom Chatterton, Ted Mapes, Jack Rockwell. Director: R. G. Springsteen.

Plainsman and the Lady: Republic 1946. 87 minutes. Wiliam Elliott, Vera Ralston, Gail Patrick, Joseph Schildkraut, Donald Barry, Andy Clyde, Raymond Walburn, Reinhold Schunzel, Paul Hurst, William B. Davidson, Charles Judels, Eva Puig, Jack Lambert, Stuart Hamblen, Noble Johnson,

Hal Taliaferro, Byron Foulger, Pierre Watkin, Eddy Waller, Charles Morton, Martin Garralaga, Guy Beach, Joseph Crehan, Grady Sutton, Eddie Parks, Norman Willis, Tex Terry, Hank Bell, Chuck Roberson, Rex Lease, Henry Wills, Jack O'Shea, Carl Sepulveda, Daniel Day Tolman, David Williams, Lola & Fernando.
Director: Joseph Kane.

Wyoming: Republic 1947. 84 minutes. William Elliott, Vera Ralston, John Carroll, George "Gabby" Hayes, Albert Dekker, Virginia Grey, Maria Ouspenskaya, Grant Withers, Harry Woods, Minna Gombell, Dick Curtis, Roy Barcroft, Trevor Bardette, Paul Harvey, Louise Kane, Linda Green, Tom London, George Chesebro, Jack O'Shea, Charles Middleton, Eddy Waller, Olin Howlin, Glenn Strange, Charles King, Eddie Acuff, Marshall Reed, Rex Lease, Charles Morton, Tex Terry, Dale Fisk, Ed Peil Sr., Roque Ybarra, James Archuletta, David Williams, Lee Shumway.
Director: Joseph Kane.

On the Republic back lot, three-year-old Linda Green, smiles at Bill Elliott during a break from the filming of WYOMING.

The Fabulous Texan: Republic 1947. 95 minutes. William Elliott, Catherine McLeod, John Carroll, Albert Dekker, Andy Devine, Jim Davis, Ruth Donnelly, Russell Simpson, James Brown, George Beban, Tommy Kelly, Johnny Sands, Harry Davenport, John Miles, Robert Coleman, Robert Barrat, Douglass Dumbrille, Reed Hadley, Roy Barcroft, Frank Ferguson, Glenn Strange, Selmer Jackson, Harry Cheshire, Harry Woods, Karl Hackett, John Hamilton, Pierre Watkin, Ed Cassidy, Tris Coffin, Stanley Andrews, Olin Howlin, Kenneth MacDonald, Jack Ingram, Ted Mapes, Pierce Lyden, Al Ferguson, Ethan Laidlaw, Ray Teal, Franklyn Farnum. Director: Edward Ludwig.

Old Los Angeles: Republic 1948. 88 minutes. William Elliott, Catherine McLeod, John Carroll, Joseph Schildkraut, Andy Devine, Paul Hurst, Estelita Rodriguez, Roy Barcroft, Joe Sawyer, Henry Brandon, Grant Withers, Virginia Brissac, Tito Renaldo, Julian Rivero, Earle Hodgins, Augie Gomez. Director: Joseph Kane.

The Gallant Legion: Republic 1948. 88 minutes. William Elliott, Adrian Booth, Joseph Schildkraut, Bruce Cabot, Andy Devine, Jack Holt, Adele Mara, Grant Withers, James Brown, Hal Taliaferro, Russell Hicks, Herbert Rawlinson, Marshall Reed, Harry Woods, Roy Barcroft, Bud Osborne, Hank Bell, Jack Ingram, George Chesebro, Noble Johnson, Rex Lease, John Hamilton, Emmett Vogan, Trevor Bardette, Gene

Adrian Booth and Bill Elliott in a publicity still for THE GALLANT LEGION (Republic, 1948).

Stutenroth, Ferris Taylor, Iron Eyes Cody, Kermit Maynard, Jack Kirk, Merrill McCormack, Fred Kohler Jr., Glenn Stange, Tex Terry, Joseph Crehan, Lester Sharpe, Peter Perkins, Cactus Mack.
Director: Joseph Kane.

The Last Bandit: Republic 1949. 80 minutes. Trucolor. William Elliott, Adrian Booth, Forrest Tucker, Andy Devine, Jack Holt, Grant Withers, Minna Gombell, Virginia Brissac, Louis Faust, Stanley Andrews, Martin Garralaga, Joseph Crehan, Charles Middleton, Rex Lease, Emmett Lynn, Gene Roth, George Chesebro, Hank Bell, Jack O'Shea, Steve Clark, Tex Terry.
Director: Joseph Kane.

Hellfire: Republic 1949. 90 minutes. Trucolor. William Elliott, Marie Windsor, Forrest Tucker, Jim Davis, H. B. Warner,

Forrest Tucker, Marie Windsor and Elliott (HELLFIRE, Republic, 1949).

Grant Withers, Paul Fix, Emory Parnell, Esther Howard, Jody Gilbert, Harry Woods, Denver Pyle, Trevor Bardette, Dewey Robinson, Harry Tyler, Hank Worden, Kenneth MacDonald, Eva Novak, Richard Alexander, Louis Faust, Edward Keane. Director: R. G. Springsteen.

The Savage Horde: Republic 1950. 90 minutes. William Elliott, Adrian Booth, Grant Withers, Jim Davis, Barbra Fuller, Noah Beery Jr., Douglass Dumbrille, Bob Steele, Will Wright, Roy Barcroft, Earle Hodgins, Stuart Hamblen, Hal Taliaferro, Lloyd Ingraham, Marshall Reed, Crane Whitley, Charles Stevens, James Flavin, Ed Cassidy, Kermit Maynard, Jack O'Shea, George Chesebro, Monte Montague, Bud Osborne, Reed Howes. Director: Joseph Kane.

The Showdown: Republic 1950. 86 minutes. William Elliott, Marie Windsor, Walter Brennan, Harry Morgan, Rhys Williams, Jim Davis, William Ching, Nacho Galindo, Leif Erickson, Henry Rowland, Charles Stevens, Victor Kilian, Yakima Canutt, Guy Teague, William Steele, Jack Sparks. Directors: Dorrell McGowan and Stuart McGowan.

The Longhorn: Monogram 1951. 70 minutes. Wild Bill Elliott, Myron Healey, Phyllis Coates, John, Marshall Reed, William Fawcett, Lee Roberts, Carol Henry, Zon Murray, Steve Clark, Lane Bradford, Herman Hack, Carl Mathews. Director: Lewis D. Collins.

Waco: Monogram 1952. 68 minutes. Wild Bill Elliott, Pamela Blake, I.Stanford Jolley, Richard Avonde, Stanley Andrews, Paul Pierce, Lane Bradford, Pierce Lyden, Terry Frost, Michael Whalen, Stanley Price, Ray Bennett, House Peters Jr., Ray Jones, Ed Cassidy, Russ Whiteman, Richard Paxton. Director: Lewis D. Collins.

Kansas Territory: Monogram 1952. 73 minutes. Wild Bill Elliott, Peggy Stewart, Lane Bradford, Marshall Reed, I. Stanford Jolley, House Peters Jr., Lyle Talbot, Terry Frost, John Hart, William Fawcett, Fuzzy Knight, Stanley Andrews, Lee Roberts, Ted Adams, Pierce Lyden. Director: Lewis D. Collins.

Fargo: Monogram 1952. 69 minutes. Wild Bill Elliott, Phyllis Coates, Myron Healey, Fuzzy Knight, Arthur Space, Robert Wilke, Jack Ingram, Terry Frost, Robert Bray, Tim Ryan, Florence Lake, Stanley Andrews, Richard Reeves, Gene Roth. Directors: Joseph Poland and Jack DeWitt.

The Maverick: Allied Artists 1952. 71 minutes. Wild Bill Elliott, Myron Healey, Phyllis Coates, Richard Reeves, Terry Frost, Rand Brooks, Russell Hicks, Robert Bray, Florence Lake, Gregg Barton, Denver Pyle, Robert Wilke, Eugene Roth, Joel Allen. Director: Thomas Carr.

The Homesteaders: Allied Artists 1953. 62 minutes.Wild Bill Elliott, Robert Lowery, Barbara Allen, Emmett Lynn, George Wallace, Buzz Henry, Rick Vallin, Stanley Price, William Fawcett, James Seay, Tom Monroe, Ray Walker. Director: Lewis D. Collins.

Rebel City: Allied Artists 1953. 62 minutes. Wild Bill Elliott, Marjorie Lord, Robert Kent, Ray Walker, I. Stanford Jolley, Keith Richards, Henry Rowland, Denver Pyle, John Crawford, Otto Waldis, Stanley Price, Michael Vallon. Director: Thomas Carr.

Topek: Allied Artists 1953. 69 minutes. Wild Bill Elliott, Phyllis Coates, Rick Vallin, Fuzzy Knight, John James, Denver Pyle, Dick Crockett, Harry Lauter, Dale Van Sickel, Ted Mapes, Henry Rowland, Edward Clark.

Director: Thomas Carr.

Vigilante Terror: Allied Artists 1953. 70 minutes. Wild Bill Elliott, Fuzzy Knight, Mary Ellen Kay, Myron Healey, I. Stanford Jolley, Henry Rowland, George Wallace, Zon Murray, Richard Avonde, Michael Colgan, Denver Pyle, Robert Bray, Al Haskell, John James.
Director: Lewis D. Collins.

Bitter Creek: Allied Artists 1954. 74 minutes. Wild Bill Elliott, Beverly Garland, Carleton Young, Veda Ann Borg, Claude Akins, John Harmon, John Pickard, Jim Hayward, Forrest Taylor, Mike Ragan, Zon Murray, John Larch, Florence Lake, Earle Hodgins, Jane Easton, Joe Devlin.
Director: Thomas Carr.

The Forty-Niners: Allied Artists 1954. 71 minutes. Wild Bill Elliott, Virginia Grey, Henry Morgan, John Doucette, Lane Bradford, I. Stanford Jolley, Denver Pyle, Ralph Sanford, Gregg Barton, Harry Lauter, Earle Hodgins.
Director: Thomas Carr.

Dial Red 0: Allied Artists 1955. 63 minutes. Bill Elliott, Keith Larson, Paul Picerni, Helen Stanley, Jack Kruschen, Elaine Riley, Robert Bice, Rick Vallin, George Eldredge, John Phillips, Regina Gleason, Rankin Mansfield, William J. Tannen, Mort Mills.
Director: Daniel B. Ullman.

Sudden Danger: Allied Artists 1955. 65 minutes. Bill Elliott, Beverly Garland, Tom Drake, Dayton Lummis, Helene Stanton, Lucien Littlefield, Minerva Urecal, Lyle Talbot, Frank Jenks, Pierre Watkin, John Close, Ralph Gamble.
Director: Hubert Cornfield.

Calling Homicide: Allied Artists 1956. 61 minutes. Bill Elliott,

Kathleen Case, Myron Healey, Dan Haggerty, Jeanne Cooper, Thomas Browne Henry, Lyle Talbot, Almira Sessions, Herb Virgran, James Best, John Dennis.
Director: Edward Bernds.

Chain of Evidence: Allied Artists 1957. 62 minutes. Bill Elliott, James Lydon, Claudia Barrett, Don Haggerty, Tina Carver, Ross Elliott, Meg Randall, Timothy Carey, John Bleifer, Dabbs Greer, John Close, Hugh Sanders.
Director: Paul Landres.

Footsteps In the Night: Allied Artists 1957. 62 minutes. Bill Elliott, Douglas Dick, Eleanore Tanin, Don Haggerty, Robert Shayne, James Flavin, Gregg Palmer, Harry Tyler, Ann Griffith, Zena Marshall.
Director: Jean Yarbrough.

A scene from FOOTSTEPS IN THE NIGHT.

Marshal of Trail City: (This was a pilot for an unsold TV series.) Century Television Productions 1950. 25 minutes. Bill Elliott, Dub Taylor, Bill Kennedy, Valley Keene, Timmy Tate, Tom Hubbard, Mildred Huntley, Bob Clark.
Directors: Norman K. Doyle and Edward C. Semmel.

More of the
AUTHOR'S FAVORITES

Ray and Maude Nance, Bill
Elliott's father and mother
(Kansas City, Missouri, 1921).

Gordon "Bill," Brother Dale,
and Sister Carmen Nance
(Kansas City, Missouri, 1921).

Wild Bill Elliott and Brother
Dale (Hollywood, California).

*We apologize for
the poor quality of
the photographs
on this page.
To the author's
knowledge,
they are the
best available.*

Bill with his first wife, Helen.

Lunch at the William Elliotts' in this unique setting is a glamourous occasion. The dining room is done in a Mexican-Modern manner, with brilliant color tones in the chairs and in the war red shutters. The wrought-iron table is topped by an antique mirror. Bill's current picture on his Republic contract is THE GALLANT LEGION.

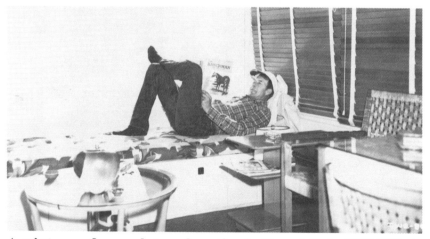

A picture of complete relaxation! Republic's Bill Elliott catches up on his reading in the cozy tea house on his Malibu Beach estate.

Who would dare face a two-gun Wild Bill Elliott?

"Everything is under control, Beaver." (VIGILANTES OF DODGE CITY, Republic, 1949).

Bill and Sonny in THE LAW COMES TO TEXAS (Columbia, 1939).

A casually-attired Elliott with his movie set chair.

Elliott, as Gary Conway in THE GALLANT LEGION (Republic, 1948).

HELLFIRE, (Republic, 1949).

With Roy Barcroft in CHEYENNE WILDCAT.

IN OLD LOS ANGELES (Republic, 1948).

Sight Seein'—Jane Withers climbs a ladder to get a good look at the sights on Columbia ranch, while Bill Elliott, cowboy star, acts as guide. Jane is appearing in HER FIRST BEAU and Bill's new picture is NORTH FROM THE LONE STAR.

Elliott with Iron Eyes Cody from the serial OVERLAND WITH KIT CARSON (Columbia, 1939).

162

One-sheet ad posters were most always used to tell us Wild Bill was coming to our local theatre.

Bill Elliott is proud of his show horse.

Bill Elliott pushing Royal Crown Cola.

Elliott presents a bouquet of flowers to his leading lady on the first day of shooting HELLFIRE. The lady, Marie Windsor, dons a man's outfit for some scenes in the movie.

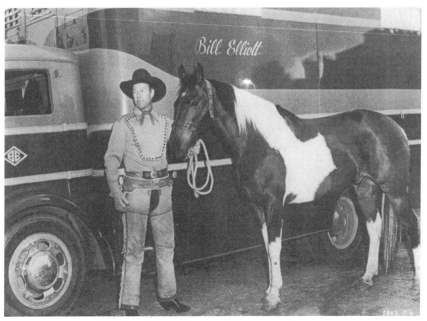

Bill and his horse Sonny on tour.

Helen Talbot, left, Bill Elliott, and Adele Mara, doing publicity
shots on the Republic Studios back lot.

Elliott holds the skein of wool for Rusty Thorsen during a lull in the filming of Republic's WYOMING. But Elliott's expression plainly tells the charming miss that she isn't fooling him a bit—he knows darned well he's been talked into something!

**Bill Elliott with Iris Meredith in OVERLAND WITH KIT
CARSON (Columbia, 1942).**

Bill Elliott with Vera Ralston in WYOMING (Republic, 1947).

Bill and an unidentified fan in Martinsville, Virginia.

Claude Ezell, of the Variety Club Charity in Dallas Texas, where Bill Elliott was doing a public appearance.

Here is a special rare photo of four giants of Republic Studios during its hay day. Left to right: Gene Autry, Herbert Yates, president of Republic Studios, Roy Rogers, and Bill Elliott.

This rare group photograph, taken in 1941, was made backstage at the Pantage Theatre, in Hollywood. Upper row: Eddie Polo, (unknown), William Desmond, Lane Chandler, John Wayne, Leo Carrillo, George Marshall, Johnny Mack Brown, Col. Tim McCoy, Yakima Canutt, Nell O'Day, Montie Montana, Kermit Maynard. Lower Row: Glen Tryon, Buck Jones, Bill Elliott, Russell Hayden, Jimmy Rogers, Big Boy Williams, Will James.

Bill Elliott, as he looked while living in LasVegas, Nevada.

ABOUT THE AUTHOR

Reared in Oak Ridge, Tennessee, Bobby Copeland began going to the Saturday matinee B-Western movies at nearby theaters. He was immediately impressed by the moral code of these films, and has tried to pattern his life after the example set by the cowboy heroes. After graduating from high school and attending Carson-Newman College and the University of Tennessee, he set out to raise a family and start a career at the Oak Ridge National Laboratory. His love for the old Western films was put on the shelf and lay dormant for some 35 years. One Saturday, in the mid-eighties, he happened to turn on his television and the station was showing a Lash LaRue picture. This rekindled his interest. He contacted the TV program's host ("Marshal" Andy Smalls), and was invited to appear on the program. Since that time, Bobby has had some 100 articles published, contributed to twelve books, made several speeches, appeared on television over 20 times, and has been interviewed by several newspapers and four independent radio stations as well as the Public Radio Broadcasting System to provide commentary and promote interest in B-Western films. In 1985 he was a co-founder of the Knoxville, Tennessee-based "Riders of the Silver Screen Club," serving five times as president. He initiated and continues to edit the club's newsletter. In 1996, his book *Trail Talk* was published by Empire Publishing, Inc. (one of the world's largest publishers of books on Western films and performers), and in 1998, he published *The Bob Baker Story*, and *The Whip Wilson Story*. He has attended some 45 Western film festivals, and met many

The author with a shirt that belonged to Bill Elliott.

of the Western movie performers. He continues to contribute articles to the various Western magazines, and he is a regular columnist for *Western Clippings*. In 1988, Bobby received the "Buck Jones Rangers Trophy," presented annually to individuals demonstrating consistent dedication to keeping the spirit of the B-Western alive. In 1994, Don Key (Empire Publishing) and Boyd Magers (Video West, Inc. & *Western Clippings*) awarded Bobby the "Buck Rainey Shoot-em-Ups Pioneer Award," which yearly honors a fan who has made significant contributions towards the preservation of interest in the B-Westerns.

Bobby is a deacon, Sunday School teacher and an usher at Oak Ridge's Central Baptist Church. He retired in 1996 after 40 years at the same workplace. Bobby plans to continue his church work, write more B-Western articles, and enjoy his retirement with his faithful sidekick, Joan.

Other Western Books Available from Empire Publishing, Inc.

ALLAN "ROCKY" LANE, REPUBLIC'S ACTION ACE by Chuck Thornton and David Rothel. The most complete tribute to Allan Lane ever published. 184 pages, more than 200 photographs., hardcover.

AN AMBUSH OF GHOSTS by David Rothel. In twelve chapters and over 350 striking then-and-now photos (sixteen pages of beautiful color), the author traces Western film history through the location sites which served to bring the old West to life in the movies. 304 pages, hardcover.

THE BOB BAKER STORY by Bobby J. Copeland. Includes a Bob Baker quiz,; *Variety* reviews, letters from Bob Baker, movie ads; filmography, and much more.

BOB STEELE STARS AND SUPPORT PLAYERS 1921 TO 1946 by Bob Nareau. This book examines more than 600 of the support players who were on the set and before the camera in those Bob Steele films of yesteryear.

BUSTER CRABBE: A SELF-PORTRAIT as told to Karl Whitezel. This autobiography of Buster Crabbe displays the heart of a true champion, molded by the hands of a loving family and forged by the disciplines needed to win.

CANDID COWBOYS, VOL. 2 by Neil Summers. Includes photos and captions on Buck Jones, John Wayne, Randolph Scott, Gene Autry, Gary Cooper, Roy Rogers, and many more.

THE COWBOY AND THE KID by J. Brim Crow III and Jack H. Smith. Explores memories of the Saturday matinee with over 230 photographs.

COWBOY MOVIE POSTERS by Bruce Hershenson. This illustrated volume of classic movie posters offers a rare look across time, at filmmakers' and film studio artists' vivid images of the Cowboy and his Wild West. Features hundreds of full-color movie posters from the early 1900s to the present.

THE DICK POWELL STORY by Tony Thomas. This is the full account of the life and career of one of the most diversely talented and interesting men ever involved in the entertainment industry. 180 pages.

DON MILLER'S HOLLYWOOD CORRAL with foreword by Gene Autry and afterword by Roy Rogers. This huge book is a comprehensive B-Western round-up. 450 photos, 560 pages., hardcover.

DUKE: THE LIFE AND IMAGE OF JOHN WAYNE by Ronald L. Davis. In this illuminating biography, Davis focuses on Wayne's human side, portraying a complex personality defined by frailty and insecurity, as well as courage and strength. Hardcover.

THE FILMS AND CAREER OF AUDIE MURPHY by Sue Gossett. 200 pages, more than 100 photos, softcover.

THE FILMS OF THE CISCO KID by Francis M. Nevins, Jr. In this book, the author covers the various transformation of Cisco: from short silent movies of the nineteen teens, all the way to the 1994 Cisco TV movie.

THE FILMS OF HOPALONG CASSIDY by Francis M. Nevins. Each of the Hopalong Cassidy movies and each episode of the Hopalong Cassidy TV series is covered in detail.

FROM PIGSKIN TO SADDLE LEATHER: THE FILMS OF JOHNNY MACK BROWN by John A. Rutherford. Includes chapters on the sidekicks, and his co-star, Tex Ritter. 212 pages, 200 photos.

THE GENE AUTRY Reference - Trivia - Scrapbook BOOK by David Rothel. This book contains all you ever wanted to know about America's Favorite Cowboy. Over 200 photos, softcover or hardcover.

THE GOLDEN CORRAL: A ROUNDUP OF MAGNIFICENT WESTERN FILMS by Ed Audreychuk. In this book, the author examines fourteen of the finest, most memorable Western films—from John Ford's *Stagecoach* (1939) to Clint Eastwood's *Unforgiven* (1992)—and shows how they have shaped and perpetuated the mythology of the Old West and its heroes.

THE HOLLYWOOD POSSE: THE STORY OF A GALLANT BAND OF HORSEMEN WHO MADE MOVIE HISTORY by Diana Serra Cary. In a rare, insider's view, the author tell the story of a handful of discarded horsemen who stumbled upon and entirely new frontier—Hollywood, and survived another fifty years as riders, stuntmen, and doubles for the stars.

THE HOXIE BOYS: The Lives and Films of Jack and Al Hoxie by Edgar M. Wyatt. This is the story of the Hoxie boys with their struggles and triumphs in real life and their experiences in motion pictures, circuses, and wild west shows.

IN A DOOR, INTO A FIGHT, OUT A DOOR, INTO A CHASE: Movie Making remembered by the Guy at the Door by William Witney. 246 pages, hardcover.

I WAS THAT MASKED MAN by Clayton Moore. Moore shares his real-life adventure of becoming an American icon. Softcover.

JOEL McCREA: RIDING THE HIGH COUNTRY by Tony Thomas. The first full account of the life and career of actor Joel McCrea. Over 200 photos.

KING COWBOY: TOM MIX AND THE MOVIES by Robert S. Birchard. The most complete annotated Mix filmography every compiled and many never-before published photographs. 280 pages.

THE LIFE AND FILMS OF BUCK JONES: THE SILENT ERA by Buck Rainey. Includes many, many photos from the author's personal collection, as well as some loaned from the Jones family.

THE LIFE AND FILMS OF BUCK JONES: THE SOUND ERA by Buck Rainey. The most complete biography of Buck Jones available. Includes many photos and a special photos scrapbook section.

MORE COWBOY MOVIE POSTERS by Bruce Hershenson. Features over 350 full color images from western films, from the earliest silents to the present day.

MORE COWBOY SHOOTING STARS by John A. Rutherford and Richard B. Smith, III. The handiest A- and B-Western book ever devised! Includes a listing of each star's films chronologically in release order with running time and studios listed for each film. Photos throughout. Hardcover.

THE REAL BOB STEELE AND A MAN CALLED BRAD by Bob Nareau. A biography of family, friends, and associates. 156 pages.

THE ROUND-UP, compiled and edited by Donald R. Key. A pictorial history of Western movie and television stars through the years. Full page photos of more than 300 stars, sidekicks, heroines, villains, and assorted players. Hardcover.

THE ROY ROGERS Reference - Trivia - Scrapbook BOOK by David Rothel. Contains all you ever wanted to know about the King of the Cowboys! Almost 200 vivid photos. Softcover.

SADDLE GALS by Edgar M. Wyatt and Steve Turner. This book is a filmography of female players in B-Westerns of the sound era. Softcover.

SADDLE PALS: A Complete B-Western Roster of the Sound Era with Complete Listing of Serials: 1930-1956, by Garv Towell and Wayne E. Keates.

TELEVISION WESTERNS: MAJOR AND MINOR SERIES, 1946-1978 by Richard West. 168 pages, softcover.

TIM HOLT by David Rothel. Here is almost everything you ever wanted to know about this great Western film star. 290 pages, hardcover.

THE TOM MIX BOOK by M. G. "Bud" Norris. Includes a detailed 336-movie filmography, a history of the Tom Mix Radio Program with descriptions of all 148 premiums, Tom's circus career and an exhaustive collector's guide to Tom Mix toys, comics, arcade cards, etc. 380 pages.

TRAIL TALK by Bobby J. Copeland. Contains quotes and comments (compiled by the author while attending almost 40 Western film conventions through the years) from those lovable and memorable participants of Western movies. 25 photos, 168 pages, softcover.

THE ULTIMATE CLINT EASTWOOD TRIVIA BOOK by Lee Pfeiffer and Michael Lewis. Features hundreds of questions based on his films. Complete with photo quiz section.

THE ULTIMATE JOHN WAYNE TRIVIA BOOK by Alvin H. Marill. 136 pages

THE UNSUNG HEROES by Neil Summers. The long-awaited book on the Hollywood stuntmen and stuntwomen by professional stuntman/actor/author Neil Summers. 128 pages, 126 photos.

WAY OUT WEST by Jane and Michael Stern. The spirit of the West is the soul of America, and this book celebrates the West as no others have done.

WHATEVER HAPPENED TO RANDOLPH SCOTT? by C. H. Scott. With this book, you can go behind the walls of this actor's Beverly Hills home and learn about his personal life. Written by Randolph Scott's only son.

THE WHIP WILSON STORY by Bobby J. Copeland. Although not a "major" Western star, Whip Wilson made 22 starring films. The author pays a wonderful tribute to this whip-cracking cowboy in this book.

WHITE HATS AND SILVER SPURS: Interviews with 24 Stars of the Film and Television Westerns of the Thirties through the Sixties. 276 pages, hardcover.

ALSO BY BOBBY COPELAND,
TRAIL TALK

Contains quotes and comments from those lovable and memorable participants of Western movies of days gone by—gone, but certainly not forgotten!

Many of the quotes were compiled, first hand, while attending almost 40 Western film conventions through the years, where actors, directors, producers and others have gathered to meet their fans!

★ CANDID COMMENTS and QUOTES by many performers and participants of THE SATURDAY MATINEE WESTERN FILMS

★ The cowboys' & cowgirls' REAL NAMES before changed by the studios!

★ The names of the MOVIE HORSES ridden by the cowboys & cowgirls!

★ Cowboy CREEDS given to youngsters to guide them down a straight trail!

★ Recent PHOTOS of Western stars met by the author at celebrity functions. . .

★ AND MUCH MORE!

Order this book today for only $12.50 *(+ $2.00 shipping)*

*   *   *

This is a worthy book to add to your collection. Some books leave you in the air as to what is going on. This is straight talk from one who really knows. Order it and Enjoy!
> —Dominick Marafioti, Natl. Chief, Buck Jones Rangers of America

Highly recommended. You can get a real feel for the stars by reading their comments about their work and their co-workers.
> —Ron Downey, World of Yesterday

*   *   *

**EMPIRE PUBLISHING
PO BOX 717
MADISON, NC 27025-0717
PH 336-427-5850
FAX 336-427-7372
EMAIL:movietv@pop.vnet.net
www.empirepublishinginc.com**

Bobby Copeland's

B-WESTERN
BOOT
HILL

A Final Tribute to the Cowboys and Cowgirls Who Rode the Saturday Matinee Movie Range

1000+ ENTRIES !

The Most Complete List Ever Assembled of Birth Dates, Death Dates, and Real Names of Those Beloved B-Western Performers.

Bobby J. Copeland has produced a literary milestone which surely will rank at the top among those important Western film history books printed within the past 30 years.

—Richard B. Smith, III

Only $15.00 (+ $2.00 shipping).

Through the years, Bobby Copeland has collected actual obituaries of hundreds of B-Western heroes, heavies, helpers, heroines and sidekicks. He is sharing them here for the first time ever. Also included is a listing of actual burial locations of many of the stars. Many photos throughout.

PO BOX 717 • MADISON, NC 27025
Ph 336-427-5850 • Fax 336-427-7372
email: movietv@pop.vnet.net

RIDING THE
(Silver Screen)
RANGE

by Ann Snuggs

This is the ULTIMATE WESTERN MOVIE TRIVIA BOOK! With this book in hand, one can become a Western movie "wizard" in a matter of days.

There are more than 1000 great questions in this fun-filled collection for the Western movie fan, spanning the '30s, '40s, '50s, through the '90s. There's even a photo trivia section!

This book is designed to ENTERTAIN, INFORM and CHALLENGE the novice as well as the diehard fan. It features more than 1000 questions covering the intriguing and entertaining Western films and television shows from the 1930s through the 1990s.

Almost everyone enjoys movies and most everyone loves Western movies. That is why just about everyone will love this book. *Order Yours Today!*

Sample Questions Include:

1. *From the John Wayne film, RIO BRAVO, what actor played the cantankerous character who was known as "Stumpy"?*

2. *Gene Autry recorded one of the most popular Christmas songs of all time. Name that tune!*

3. *From the 1960s, what was the first Western flick to receive an "R" rating?*

4. *What actor portrayed the "Durango Kid" character during the 1940s and 1950s?*

5. *What major star turned down the offer to play "Matt Dillon" on televsion series GUNSMOKE, but recommended a friend for the part?*

6. *Name the Country Music singer who co-starred with Kirk Douglas in THE GUNFIGHT.*

MORE THAN 1000 MORE QUESTIONS with ANSWERS!

Send only **$15.00** (+$2.00 shipping) **to:**
EMPIRE PUBLISHING, INC. • BOX 717 •MADISON, NC 27025-0717

AN AMBUSH OF GHOSTS

A Personal Guide to Favorite Western Film Locations

by David Rothel

AN AMBUSH OF GHOSTS
A Personal Guide to Favorite Western Film Locations

by David Rothel

You'll see fascinating then-and-now photos, travelers' easy-to-follow directions to all the sites, and discover where to look and what to look for at these 20 locations:

TEXAS:
Alamo Village

CALIFORNIA
Bronson Canyon
Vasquez Rocks
Red Rock Canyon
Lone Pine
Big Bear
Pioneertown
Corriganville
Iverson's Ranch
Golden Oak Ranch
Andy Jauregui Ranch
Melody Ranch
Columbia Ranch
Republic Back Lot
Universal Back Lot

ARIZONA
Old Tucson

UTAH
Monument Valley

NEW MEXICO
Cook Ranch
Eaves Ranch
Bonanza Creek

This book has been featured by Leonard Maltin on *Entertainment Tonight* on two occasions. It has received favorable reviews by Grady Franklin (*The Indianapolis News*), Walt Belcher (*The Tampa Tribune*), Dorothy Stockbridge (*The Sarasota Herald-Tribune*), and the "Bunkhouse Bookshelf" in *The Western Horseman*.

In twelve chapters and over 350 striking then-and-now photos **(16 pages in beautiful color)**, Rothel traces Western film history through the location sites which served to bring the old West to life in movies. Rothel spent three years researching the locations and another year writing this comprehensive book.

$40⁰⁰
(+ $3⁰⁰ shipping)

EMPIRE PUBLISHING
PO BOX 717
MADISON, NC 27025

PH 336-427-5850
FAX 336-427-7372

Richard Boone

"A Knight without Armor in a Savage Land"

Here is just about everything you ever wondered about one of America's favorite actors

- MILESTONES AND MINUTIAE

- IN-DEPTH INTERVIEWS WITH FAMILY MEMBERS

- IN-DEPTH INTERVIEWS WITH FRIENDS AND CO-WORKERS:

- THE WIT AND WISDOM OF RICHARD BOONE.

- *MEDIC* Episode Guide.

- *HAVE GUN, WILL TRAVEL* Episode Guide.

- *THE RICHARD BOONE SHOW* Episode Guide.

- *HEC RAMSEY* Episode Guide.

- TV MOVIES & ANTHOLOGY TV PROGRAMS Episode Guide.

* *SPECIAL BOOK BONUS:* Each copy of *RICHARD BOONE, "A Knight without Armor in a Savage Land"* is packaged (at no extra cost) with a Johnny Western CD featuring "The Ballad of Paladin" and "The Guns of Rio Muerto," the only commercial recording Richard Boone made.

FREE Johnny Western CD included with each book!

ORDER YOUR COPY NOW!

only **$35.00** postpaid

Includes *FREE* Johnny Western CD

EMPIRE PUBLISHING, INC • PO BOX 717 • MADISON, NC 27025-0717

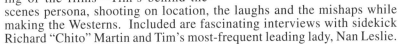
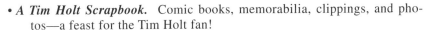

THE GENE AUTRY

Reference-Trivia-Scrapbook

BOOK

by David Rothel

HERE IS EVERYTHING YOU EVER WANTED TO KNOW ABOUT AMERICA'S FAVORITE SINGING COWBOY, GENE AUTRY!

- **One Man's Life—Another Man's Trivia.** A giant, comprehensive compendium of questions and answers—little-known facts about a well-known cowboy.
- **The Wit and Wisdom of Gene Autry.** Memorable quotes on a wide range of subjects.
- **The Films of Gene Autry.** A complete Filmography!
- **Gene Autry on Tour.** Gene, Champion, and a whole entourage of entertainers played as many as 85 dates on a single tour. The stories they have to tell!
- **Gene Autry—On the Record.** A complete discography!
- **"The Gene Autry Show" TV Series.** This is the FIRST publication of the credits for Gene Autry's TV Series—ALL 91 episodes!
- **"Melody Ranch Theater."** During the 1980s, Gene was back on TV hosting his classic Western films.
- **The Autry Museum of Western Heritage**—Gene's long-time dream comes true!

ALL OF THIS AND MUCH MORE!

Author David Rothel is a Western film historian who has also written *The Singing Cowboy Stars, Who Was that Masked Man? The Story of the Lone Ranger, The Great Show Business Animals, Those Great Cowboy Sidekicks, The Roy Rogers Book, An Ambush of Ghosts,* and *Tim Holt.*

- 278 pages
- Full color cover
- Hundreds of photos
- $25.00 (+$3.00 shipping)

SEND ORDERS TO:

EMPIRE PUBLISHING, INC.
PO BOX 717
MADISON, NC 27025-0717

THE ROY ROGERS
Reference-Trivia-Scrapbook
BOOK
by David Rothel

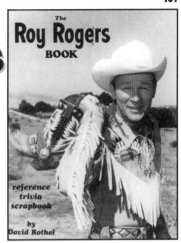

HERE IS EVERYTHING YOU EVER WANTED TO KNOW ABOUT "THE KING OF THE COWBOYS," ROY ROGERS!

THE FILMS AND CAREER OF AUDIE MURPHY

by Sue Gossett

Film-by-film synopses of this legendary Hollywood Star / War Hero

This book reflects all of Audie Murphy's movie career of 44 films. Also included are two of his three made-for-television movies and one episode of his 1961 series, "Whispering Smith."

Along with acting and producing films, Audie's brilliant and well-documented war record is highlighted for those who want a thumb-nail account of what he endured while in the service of his country. This young man was not yet old enough to vote when he was awarded every combat medal for valor this nation had to offer.

Audie Murphy loved country music and expressed himself through the lyrics of dozens of songs, some of which were recorded by famous artists. Some of his poetry and songs are included in a special chapter. Order today!

- 200 pages
- Full color cover
- More than 100 photos
- **$18.00** (+$2.00 shipping)

SEND ORDERS TO:

EMPIRE PUBLISHING, INC.
PO BOX 717
MADISON, NC 27025-0717

Phone 336-427-5850 • Fax 336-427-7372 • Email: movietv@pop.vnet.net

RANDOLPH SCOTT/ A FILM BIOGRAPHY

by Jefferson Brim Crow, III

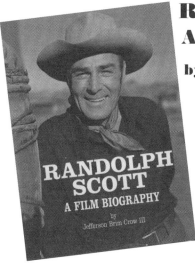

This book contains the only complete biography of this legendary star.

- Over 250 photographs
- 302 pages
- Softcover

$25.00 (+ $3⁰⁰ shipping)

WHATEVER HAPPENED TO RANDOLPH SCOTT?

by C. H. Scott

This is not just another book about a movie actor who made it to the glamour and glitz of the Hollywood scene. It is a love story that reveals the respect and admiration of a son for his father. Upon reading this narrative, one will experience growing up in the home of Randolph Scott, through the eyes of his son, Chris. As the reader begins to grieve the loss of one of Hollywood's finest stars, the answer to the question, *Whatever Happened to Randolph Scott?* will fill the heart with hope . . . he lives on in those who loved him. Includes many rare, personal photos.

$12.95 (+ $2⁰⁰ shipping)

PO Box 717 • Madison, NC 27025-0717
phone 336-427-5850 • fax 336-427-7372

EMPIRE PUBLISHING INC.

190

> "This book brings back memories for me... makes me think back to those days at Republic."
> —Monte Hale

Relive those treasured Saturday afternoons of your youth when you cheered on your favorite B-Western cowboy heroes; Tom Mix, Hoot Gibson, Ken Maynard, Tim McCoy, Gene Autry, Dale Evans, Roy Rogers, Lash LaRue, the Durango Kid, Buck Jones, Hopalong Cassidy, Wild Bill Elliott, Sunset Carson. And bring back memories of the Classic TV-Western cowboys and the more recent A-Western stars.

They're all here in what may be the mot comprehensive (and attractive) Western star picture book ever produced. You get 298 heroes, heroines, stuntmen, side-kicks, villains, and cattlepunchers, plus 2 musical groups (the Cass County Boys and the Sons of the Pioneers).

From old-time stuntman Art Acord to Tony Young (who played Cord in TV's *Gunslinger),* from Harry Carey to Clint Eastwood, this handsome volume in-cludes all your favorites from the turn of the century through the 1990s, arranged in alphabetical order for easy reference.

But this is more than just a pictorial. Each full-page entry includes a discretely placed one-paragraph background summary of the actor of group, with dates of birth and death. PLUS you get all these EXTRAS:

* Foreword by Monte Hale
* Afterword by Neil Summers
* Bibliography
* "The Western Film—Past and Present" by Ronald C. Butler
* Quality hardcover to withstand repeated use.

$35⁰⁰
(+ $3⁰⁰ shipping)

> As time marches on, and so many of our screen and per-sonal friends leave us, books like *The Round-Up* become even more important to us and to the history of Westerns.
> —Neil Summers

Empire Publishing, Inc. • Box 717 • Madison NC 27025-0717

MORE COWBOY
SHOOTING
STARS

by
John A. Rutherford
and
Richard B. Smith, III

What is it?
It's a hardcover reference book that contains almost every Western film produced from 1930 through 1992 — The B's, The A's — they all are included.

How many titles are listed?
7,267 entries in all.

Are there photographs in the book?
Yes, 105 cowboy and cowgirl pictures are within.

How are the movies listed?
This reference book has each Western film star listed with each of their films in chronological order.

What is the price and where may I order it?
Regular price is $18.00; However, if you mention you saw this ad in the *Bill Elliott: The Peaceable Man,* by Bobby Copeland, we are offering **$5.00 off** so you may order this book for **only $13.00** plus $3.00 shipping.

Hardcover; 214 pages.

192

New Offering from Empire Publishing:

MOVIE ADS
FROM THE PAST :

A Classic Collection of Movie Advertising from the '40s and '50s

This book is a nice collector's item. It has 80 pages and 450 total illustrations, including 150 ads from Western films.

Western Ads Include:
Monte Hale
Wild Bill Elliott
George Montgomery
Roy Rogers
Allan Rocky Lane
Tim Holt
Randolph Scott
Rex Allen
Charles Starrett
Joel McCrea
Gene Autry
Clayton Moore
Bill Elliott
Tex Ritter
George O'Brien
Whip Wilson
Gary Cooper
Rory Calhoun
Johnny Mack Brown
Rod Cameron
Lash LaRue

PLUS:
Boston Blackie
Bowery Boys
Elvis
Jungle Jim
Superman
John Wayne
Tarzan
James Stewart
Bogart
Dick Tracy
Rock Hudson
Jane Russell
Boris Karloff
Abbott & Costello
Ma & Pa Kettle
Martin & Lewis
Erroll Flynn
Bob Hope
Mickey Rooney
Audie Murphy
Elizabeth Taylor

ALSO:
More Westerns
Comedies
Dramas
Science Fiction
Serials

ONLY $10.00 postpaid!

Order from:

EMPIRE PUBLISHING INC

PO BOX 717 MADISON, NC 27025
Ph 336-427-5850
Fax 336-427-7372
email: movietv@pop.vnet.net

We accept Visa, Mastercard, Discover, and American Express.